The Art
of the Middle English Lyric

Essays in Criticism

The Art
of the Middle English Lyric

Essays in Criticism

Edmund Reiss

University of Georgia Press, Athens

LIBRARY OF CONGRESS CATALOG CARD NUMBER: 74–169948
INTERNATIONAL STANDARD BOOK NUMBER: 0–8203–0279–1

THE UNIVERSITY OF GEORGIA PRESS, ATHENS 30601

PRINTED IN THE UNITED STATES OF AMERICA
BY HERITAGE PRINTERS, INC.
CHARLOTTE, NORTH CAROLINA

To My Mother and My Father
who have always cared

Contents

Preface

THE ANALYSES of seven of the poems discussed here appeared earlier in somewhat different form in *College English* ("Nou goth sonne vnder wod," "Foweles in the frith," and "Wel, hwa sal thir hornes blau"), *Annuale Mediaevale* ("Myrie it is while sumer ilast" and "Wynter wakeneth al my care"), and *Style* ("Naueth my saule bute fur and ys" and "Gold and al this werdis wyn"). I am pleased to thank Gail M. Gibson for her help with research, and Dorothy E. Roberts, Evelyn M. O'Neal, and Doris O. Bailey for their assistance in preparing the manuscript. I am also grateful to my students, who over several years have freely questioned my ideas. I am delighted to thank my wife, Louise, for her many aids and comforts. And I thank the National Council of Teachers of English and the editors of the journals for permission to reprint.

In printing the lyrics, I have modernized punctuation and capitalization and have normalized the following graphemes: for þ and ð I have used *th*; for ƿ I have substituted *w*; for ȝ I have used *y* or *gh*, once *h* (ȝwas), and once *th* (souȝ); for *j*, representing a vowel, I have substituted *i*; and for initial *ff*, I have read *f*. Otherwise, I have retained the original orthography. I have made a few silent emendations, which are discussed in the essays; and several times in the discussions I have suggested other emendations not shown in the given texts.

In the bibliographic material following the poems, I have noted the most important and most easily accessible editions and critical commentaries.

Durham, North Carolina
May 1970

Introduction

THE MIDDLE ENGLISH LYRIC has recently been enjoying a scholarly and critical interest that may finally result in its being properly understood and valued. For years overshadowed by its Latin, Provençal, French, Italian, and German counterparts, these English poems, from the thirteenth through the fifteenth centuries, have failed to receive the critical attention they merit. According to M. J. C. Hodgart, "The English medieval lyric, religious and secular, is a poor relation of the splendid Continental art-form, through which many of the finest writers of the Middle Ages said what they felt most deeply."[1] As is implied here, part of the problem may be that most of these poems are anonymous, and we know of no Middle English lyricist who can act as an equivalent to such great continental lyric writers as the Archpoet, Marcabru, Guido Cavalcanti, and Walther von der Vogelweide. Lacking at least one major figure who could provide a focal point for study, the medieval English lyric form has been judged as inadequate; and on the whole the poems have interested mainly antiquaries, bibliographers, and philologists.

The second reason for the general neglect of this genre may be seen in W. T. H. Jackson's brief evaluation, that the medieval English lyric has "a pleasing naiveté and simple charm, but also a monotony of theme and lack of technical skill."[2] Such comments as this confuse surface sophistication with literary merit and reveal a prejudice linking good medieval lyric poetry with courtly tradition. But few Middle English lyrics are courtly; most are in what Charles Muscatine has termed the bourgeois tradition.[3] The poems are by and large homely, moralistic, sometimes didactic, frequently bawdy, and mostly lacking in noteworthy intricacies of form and verse technique. Still, even though the subjects and methods may not stand out or be fashionable, the poems themselves are often exciting, compel-

---

1. "Medieval Lyrics and the Ballads," in *The Age of Chaucer*, ed. Boris Ford, rev. ed. (Baltimore, 1959), p. 159.

2. *The Literature of the Middle Ages* (New York, 1960), p. 275.

3. *Chaucer and the French Tradition* (Berkeley and Los Angeles, 1957), pp. 58ff.

ling, even memorable, and clearly deserve more close study than they have received. Such examination is the best refutation of pronouncements like that made recently by Rossell Hope Robbins, that these lyrics are generally of little literary interest or value.[4]

Serious scholarly study of these lyrics may be said to have begun in the 1930s with the Oxford editions by Carleton Brown and Richard L. Greene.[5] While these editions are fundamental to a study of these poems, there was little critical appreciation before the 1950s. This decade began with three significant works: Leo Spitzer's explication of three lyrics, George Kane's evaluation of selected religious poems, and Arthur K. Moore's book-length appreciation, *The Secular Lyric in Middle English*.[6] But, even though combined with E. K. Chambers's study of the carol and the fifteenth-century lyric, G. L. Brook's edition of the Harley lyrics, and R. H. Robbins's edition of secular lyrics,[7] these works did not act as any sort of vanguard to further critical or scholarly activity.

It was only in the 1960s with the publication of Stephen Manning's works, first his important essay on "I syng of a myden," showing the richness of this poem, and then his book, *Wisdom and Number: Toward a Critical Appraisal of the Middle English Religious Lyric*,[8] that there really began to be a renaissance of studies of this poetry. Manning's highly perceptive work might have stood out as an isolated phenomenon, however, had it not been for the publication in the following years of two collections of the lyrics, by R. T. Davies

---

4. "A Highly Critical Approach to the Middle English Lyric," *CE*, 30 (1968), 75.

5. Brown, *Religious Lyrics of the XIVth Century* (1924), *English Lyrics of the XIIIth Century* (1932), *Religious Lyrics of the XVth Century* (1939); Greene, *The Early English Carols* (1935). These followed upon such earlier editions as Karl Bödekker, ed., *Altenglische Dichtungen des MS. Harl. 2253* (Berlin, 1878); E. K. Chambers and F. Sidgwick, eds., *Early English Lyrics, Amorous, Divine, Moral, and Trivial* (London, 1907); and Alexander Müller, ed., *Mittelenglische geistliche und weltliche Lyrik des XIII Jahrhunderts* (Halle, 1911); as well as F. A. Patterson, *The Middle English Penitential Lyric* (New York, 1911).

6. Spitzer, *"Explication de Texte* Applied to Three Great Middle English Poems," *ArL*, 3 (1951), 1–22, 137–65; Kane, "The Middle English Religious Lyrics," in his *Middle English Literature* (London, 1951), pp. 104–81; Moore, Lexington, Ky., 1951.

7. Chambers, *English Literature at the Close of the Middle Ages* (Oxford, 1945), pp. 66–121; Brook, *The Harley Lyrics: The Middle English Lyrics of MS. Harley 2253* (Manchester, 1948); Robbins, *Secular Lyrics of the XIVth and XVth Centuries* (Oxford, 1952).

8. "I syng of a Myden," *PMLA*, 75 (1960), 8–12; *Wisdom and Number* (Lincoln, Neb., 1962); see also the dissertation by Theo Stemmler, *Die englischen Liebesgedichte des MS. Harley 2253* (Bonn, 1962).

and by Robert D. Stevick.[9] These volumes, in paperback, made a good selection of these poems available for the first time to readers other than medievalists and for use in the classroom. Several articles in the mid-1960s attest to the renewed interest in these lyrics: along with several analyses of individual poems, there appeared a few essays—by Ruta Sikora, Robert D. Stevick, and Edmund Reiss[10]—demonstrating the literary artistry of these poems in general and showing how they can be read as works of literature, meaningful both in the Middle Ages and today.

There then appeared in quick succession two book-length studies of the lyrics, the first, Rosemary Woolf's *The English Religious Lyric in the Middle Ages*, examining in particular the relationship of the poems to late medieval contemplative meditations;[11] and the second, Sarah Appleton Weber's *Theology and Poetry in the Middle English Lyric: A Study of Sacred History and Aesthetic Form*, analyzing the poems in terms of the liturgy.[12] But while these books are interesting and valuable for understanding the historical and religious bases of the lyric, they are not much concerned with examining the artistic achievement of the poems themselves. They certainly do not do what Stevick had called for in 1966, when he spoke of the critics' "uncertainty about how to deal directly with the poems." Specifically, Stevick had insisted that we must learn "how to to talk about the poems instead of the (anonymous) poets, how to treat the texts as texts rather than as relics merely to be preserved and venerated, how to analyze the structuring of expression (the poems are linguistic utterances of a special kind) more deeply than for tropes, rhyme schemes, and metrical feet."[13] It is primarily with these thoughts in mind that I have written this book.[14]

---

9. Davies, *Medieval English Lyrics: A Critical Anthology* (London, 1963); Stevick, *One Hundred Middle English Lyrics* (Indianapolis, 1964); also Henry A. Person, ed., *Cambridge Middle English Lyrics*, rev. ed. (Seattle, 1962); and R. L. Greene, ed., *A Selection of English Carols* (Oxford, 1962).

10. Sikora, "The Structural Simplicity of the Early Middle English Lyric: Three Examples," *KN*, 11 (1964), 233–42; Stevick, "The Criticism of Middle English Lyrics," *MP*, 64 (1966), 103–17; Reiss, "A Critical Approach to the Middle English Lyric," *CE*, 27 (1966), 373–79.

11. Oxford, 1968.

12. Columbus, Ohio, 1969.

13. *MP*, 64 (1966), 117.

14. Raymond Oliver's *Poems without Names: The English Lyric, 1250–1500* (Berkeley and Los Angeles, 1970) was published while this book was in press. While it is concerned with the "stylistic coherence" of the Middle English lyric, it generally uses the poems to illustrate a technique or method and makes only brief comments about the poems themselves.

I have tried to understand what these poems are doing as pieces of literary art, as compositions having a particular relevance to an audience in the late Middle Ages and also a special interest for readers of poetry in the late twentieth century. More specifically, I have chosen twenty-five poems representing the range of Middle English lyrical poetry from the thirteenth through the fifteenth centuries. While I have not been especially concerned with being representative, the poems I have selected do illustrate various themes and techniques notable in this verse. Whereas these twenty-five poems represent the best of what is extant, they are by no means the only good or the only interesting poems in the corpus. It would have been possible to present a completely different group of lyrics that exhibit as well as these the range and achievement possible in this poetry. These, however, have the double advantage of being short and of being, by and large, well known and much discussed. Also they are, admittedly, those which I find especially interesting and about which I had something I wanted to say.

In my examination I have made use of as many critical and scholarly tools as I could justifiably employ. I have tried to understand the poems in their historical context, especially in terms of the religious meanings that are inherent in them and that provide the basis of much of their imagery. I have also endeavored to relate the symbolic language to statements by theological *auctoritees*, to the language of contemporary vernacular literature, and, when pertinent, to the iconography of late medieval art. I have concentrated on seeing how the poems do what they do and how all their parts contribute to the whole. Along with using the customary methods of close analysis—rarely applied to medieval verse—to understand poetic structure, verse technique, and wordplay, I have also made use of the principles and insights of those present-day linguists interested in stylistics. In all, I have tried to reveal the themes and forms manifest in these poems, as well as the necessary relationship between them.

My practice has been to approach each poem according to its individual demands, and I have therefore concentrated my discussion on what seems most pertinent to understanding the piece. In like manner, when a lyric is especially interesting because of its prosody, its syntax, or its religious symbolism, for instance, my analysis emphasizes these aspects. Because of this procedure, certain discussions are necessarily more technical or more theological than others. At the same time, such emphasis should be viewed as an extension of the general analysis. Whereas these extensions may appeal most to the professional critic and medieval scholar, the greater part of my discussions is aimed at the nonspecialist, including the reader coming to the Middle English lyric for the first time. As the book has been conceived and assembled, the essays may be read seriatum, but need not be. Although the poems are arranged in a general chronological order, from the thirteenth through the fifteenth centuries, they may be read in any order. When, in a few instances, one lyric is compared or contrasted with another, it is with the lyric immediately preceding the one under discussion.

While my concern has been with the particular poems and not with generic concepts or chronological developments, a few generalities may be in order. First, the distinction between secular and religious, at least insofar as the medieval lyric is concerned, seems to be both artificial and inadequate, and often something that gets in the way of understanding the various poems. Such a dichotomy focuses wholly on the surface, the *littera*, of the work and, intentionally or not, makes that represent the work itself. Most frequently, even when the surface of the poem appears to be secular, there exists beneath it a moral or religious *sentence* that represents the poem's essential significance.

Second, the lyrics seem to be more complex than is generally realized, in terms of both their methods and their meanings. Even when they are relatively simple, the simplicity is the result of perfect economy rather than of naiveté or artistic inadequacy. Often symbolism exists in these poems to create a parody of sorts: that is, the subject at hand—unreligious or irreligious as it might often appear to be—may call up or appeal to a religious background or idea that serves in turn to give the subject point and, frequently, to function as the ultimate theme or meaning of the work. A so-called courtly love situation, for example, may echo the Song of Songs, thereby calling up an ideal of Christian love—an ideal that both shows the inadequacy of the courtly love and suggests its remedy. On the subject of symbolism, it may also be noted that allegorical details are found most frequently in the longer poems and in the later verse. Likewise, symbolic parallels in the visual arts are more abundant for the fourteenth- and fifteenth-century lyrics than for the thirteenth-century ones.

Third, the lyrics are far more conventional than individual, even though they may be more personal than their continental cousins. While seeming to represent an individual poet's joy or lamentation, they pertain most of all to conventions of rhetoric, genre, and theology that have parallels in other vernacular and Latin poetry. And this is as it should be, for the medieval writer penned his rhymes to

reveal the eternal truths of which he was aware. The whole justification for his art was that by delighting he could instruct others in
these truths. Such a concept follows St. Augustine's words on the
function of *eloquentia,* words that were definitive for the Middle
Ages: "to teach, in order to instruct; to please, in order to hold; and
also, assuredly, to move, in order to convince."[15] Following Cicero,
Augustine insisted that the proper concerns of Christian art were
docere, delectare, flectere, or, alternately, *probare, delectare, movere.*
And Christian art, especially the art of the Middle Ages, was necessarily a celebration of the divine, though it may properly include an
examination of nature and man, the handiwork, as it were, of God the
artist. Medieval art is also, in this sense, an *imitatio Dei;* and though,
from a Neoplatonic or Augustinian point of view, it must necessarily
be inadequate, it can still give intimations of the immortality and
bliss in store at the end of this life for him who has lived well, as
well as insights into the hardships of this world marked by fortune,
with its necessary mutability and instability. On the one hand, taking
as their subject that which appears to be irrational and chaotic in this
world and in man, these poems show the point and meaning of life.
On the other hand, the poems frequently call up the religious ideals
and suggest a mystical union between man and God.

While my analyses have necessarily revealed the aesthetic, as well
as various archetypal, mythical, and Christian, significances of these
poems, I recognize the validity of Ananda Coomaraswamy's comparison of the medieval artist to the modern mathematician.[16] Neither possesses artistic self-consciousness, at least not in the modern
sense of the term; feeling, as such—that which is the basis of the term
"aesthetic"—is necessarily irrelevant to their works; and, most important, both are primarily concerned with economy of expression. That
is, the artist's work is most like the mathematician's formula in the
sense that each tries to reveal the greatest amount of truth in the
smallest amount of space and with the fewest number of lines or
words. The main value of both the formula and the work of art lies in
the plethora of meanings, the implications and ramifications, that are
present, and in the ability to communicate or make meaningful their
truths. Still, the brilliance of many of these short verses makes us
aware of what Peter Dronke has termed "their sharp but supple language"; and we cannot help but want to see how they create their

---

15. *De doctrina Christiana,* IV. 12–13.
16. *Christian and Oriental Philosophy of Art,* formerly titled *Why Exhibit
Works of Art?* (New York, 1956), pp. 144–45.

"moments of magnetic vitality and concentration."[17] To do so, and subsequently to analyze the poems, is to acknowledge both their emotional impact and their artistic merit, and to justify, as it were, their effectiveness to an age far removed in time and in world view from that which produced them.

---

17. *The Medieval Lyric* (New York, 1968), p. 70.

General Abbreviations

Bennett and Smithers   Bennett, J. A. W., and Smithers, G. V., eds. *Early Middle Verse and Prose.* 2d ed. Oxford: Clarendon Press, 1968.

Brook   Brook, G. L., ed. *The Harley Lyrics: The Middle English Lyrics of MS. Harley 2253.* 2d ed. Manchester: Manchester University Press, 1956.

Brown, *13*   Brown, Carleton, ed. *English Lyrics of the XIIIth Century.* Oxford: Clarendon Press, 1932.

Brown, *Rel 14*   Brown, Carleton, ed. *Religious Lyrics of the XIVth Century.* 2d ed. Revised by G. V. Smithers. Oxford: Clarendon Press, 1952.

Brown, *Rel 15*   Brown, Carleton, ed. *Religious Lyrics of the XVth Century.* Oxford: Clarendon Press, 1939.

Chambers and Sidgwick   Chambers, E. K., and Sidgwick, F., eds. *Early English Lyrics: Amorous, Divine, Moral and Trivial.* London: A. H. Bullen, 1907.

Davies   Davies, R. T., ed. *Medieval English Lyrics: A Critical Anthology.* London: Faber and Faber, 1963.

Dickins and Wilson   Dickins, Bruce, and Wilson, R. M., eds. *Early Middle English Texts.* 2d ed. Cambridge: Bowes and Bowes, 1952.

Dreves   Dreves, G. M., and Blume, C., eds. *Analecta Hymnica Medii Aevi.* Leipzig: Fues's Verlag (O. R. Reisland), 1886–1922.

Dronke, *ML*   Dronke, Peter. *The Medieval Lyric.* New York: Harper and Row, 1969.

Greene, *EEC*   Greene, Richard L., ed. *The Early Eng-
                            lish Carols.* Oxford: Clarendon Press,
                            1935.

Greene, *SEC*   Greene, R. L., ed. *A Selection of Eng-
                            lish Carols.* Oxford: Clarendon Press,
                            1962.

Index   Brown, Carleton, and Robbins, R. H.
                            The Index of Middle English Verse.
                            New York: Columbia University
                            Press, 1943.

Kane   Kane, George. "The Middle English
                            Religious Lyrics," in his *Middle Eng-
                            lish Literature.* London: Methuen,
                            1951, pp. 104–81.

Manning, *CL*   Manning, Stephen. "Game and Earnest
                            in the Middle English and Provençal
                            Love Lyrics," *Comparative Litera-
                            ture,* 18 (1966), 225–40.

Manning, *Wisdom*   Manning, Stephen. *Wisdom and Num-
                            ber: Toward a Critical Appraisal of
                            the Middle English Religious Lyric.*
                            Lincoln, Nebraska: University of
                            Nebraska Press, 1962.

Moore   Moore, Arthur K. *The Secular Lyric in
                            Middle English.* Lexington, Ken-
                            tucky: University of Kentucky Press,
                            1951.

Oliver   Oliver, Raymond. *Poems without
                            Names: The English Lyric, 1200–
                            1500.* Berkeley and Los Angeles:
                            University of California Press, 1970.

Reiss, *AnM*   Reiss, Edmund. "The Art of the Mid-
                            dle English Lyric: Two Poems on
                            Winter," *Annuale Mediaevale,* 11
                            (1970), 22–34.

Reiss, *CE*   Reiss, Edmund. "A Critical Approach
                            to the Middle English Lyric," *Col-
                            lege English,* 27 (1966), 373–79.

Reiss, *Style*   Reiss, Edmund. "Religious Common-
                            places and Poetic Artistry in the

Middle English Lyric," *Style*, 4 (1970), 97–106.

Robbins, *Sec*   Robbins, Rossell Hope, ed. *Secular Lyrics of the XIVth and XVth Centuries*. Oxford: Clarendon Press, 1952.

Sikora, *KN*   Sikora, Ruta. "The Structural Simplicity of the Early Middle English Lyric: Three Examples," *Kwartalnik Neofilologiczny*, 11 (1964), 233–42.

Sisam   Sisam, Kenneth, ed. *Fourteenth Century Verse and Prose*, corr. ed. Oxford: Clarendon Press, 1955.

Speirs   Speirs, John. *Medieval English Poetry: The Non-Chaucerian Tradition*. London: Faber and Faber, 1957.

Spitzer, *ArL*   Spitzer, Leo. *"Explication de texte* Applied to Three Great Middle English Poems," *Archivum Linguisticum*, 3 (1951), 1–22, 137–65.

Stevick, *MP*   Stevick, Robert D. "The Criticism of Middle English Lyrics," *Modern Philology*, 64 (1966), 103–17.

Stevick, *One*   Stevick, Robert D., ed. *One Hundred Middle English Lyrics*. Indianapolis: Bobbs-Merrill, 1964.

Supplement   Robbins, R. H., and Cutler, J. L. *Supplement to the Index of Middle English Verse*. Lexington, Kentucky: University of Kentucky Press, 1965.

Wells   Wells, John E. *A Manual of Writings in Middle English, 1050–1400*, with supplements 1–9. New Haven: Connecticut Academy of Arts and Sciences, 1916–1951.

Wilson, *Early*   Wilson, R. M. *Early Middle English Literature*, 2d ed. London: Methuen, 1951.

Wilson, *Lost*   Wilson, R. M. *The Lost Literature of*

| | *Medieval England*, 2d ed. London: Methuen, 1952. |
| Woolf | Woolf, Rosemary. *The English Religious Lyric in the Middle Ages.* Oxford: Clarendon Press, 1968. |

Abbreviations of Journals and Series

AnM	*Annuale Mediaevale*
ArL	*Archivum Linguisticum*
CE	*College English*
CL	*Comparative Literature*
EETS ES	Early English Text Society, Extra Series
EETS OS	Early English Text Society, Original Series
ELH	*Journal of English Literary History*
ELN	*English Language Notes*
KN	*Kwartalnik Neofilologiczny*
MED	*Middle English Dictionary*
MGH	Monumenta Germaniae Historica
MLN	*Modern Language Notes*
MLR	*Modern Language Review*
MP	*Modern Philology*
N&Q	*Notes and Queries*
OED	*Oxford English Dictionary*
PG	*Patrologia Graeca*, ed. Migne
PL	*Patrologia Latina*, ed. Migne
PLL	*Papers on Language and Literature*
PMLA	*Publications of the Modern Language Association*
TLS	*Times* (London) *Literary Supplement*
ZAA	*Zeitschrift für Anglistik und Amerikanistik*

The Art
of the Middle English Lyric

Essays in Criticism

Myrie it is while sumer ilast,
With fugheles song;
Oc nu necheth windes blast
4 And weder strong.
Ei! ei! what this nicht is long;
And ich, wid wel michel wrong,
Soregh and murne and fast.

Bodl. MS 14755 (formerly Rawlinson G. 22), fol. lv,
Index, no. 2163, p. 340; *Supplement*, p. 248.

Editions:
  Brown, 13, no. 7, p. 14.
  Chambers and Sidgwick, no. 1, p. 3.
  Davies, no. 2, p. 51.
  Stevick, *One*, no. 2, p. 3.
  Dickins and Wilson, p. 118.
  Bennett and Smithers, p. 111.

Criticism:
  Moore, p. 29.
  Reiss, *AnM*, pp. 22–28.

THIS SHORT POEM, which has come down to the present complete with its music, may well be the oldest known song in the English language. But whatever its musical accompaniment—or lack of accompaniment—it still exists as a linguistic structure that demands to be understood in terms of its content and its use of language.

The seven lines reveal a natural two-part division: lines 1–4 represent a statement in two contrastive sections—summer and winter—separated by the conjunction *oc* (but, 3); and lines 5–7 represent the narrator's response to the situation stated in the first part. Part one concerns the environment outside the narrator; he, the *ich* of the poem, is not mentioned until line 6. From a situation of cheerful unconcern, represented by summer and the birds' song, the poem moves to one of frustrating discomfort, represented by winter and the wind's blast. The last three lines comment on this discomfort, revealing it in terms of man's condition in this world, but implying also that it is based on the realization and memory of the pleasant times that once were.

The poem, while talking about the plight of an individual, is doing more than presenting the response of a thirteenth-century Englishman to cold weather. The sorrow at the end seems too extreme to be merely a response to bad weather. The long night is shown to be upon man because of *wel michel wrong* (6), and his actions of sorrowing, mourning, and fasting may be viewed as acts of penance. What is suggested here is the salvation necessary for postlapsarian man in his state of sin with its accompanying lack of spiritual light. The sorrowful cry, *Ei! ei!* (5), which has taken the place of the melodious *fugheles song* (2), is the cry of the tormented soul, the melancholy man lacking in hope and faith, suffering the dark night of the soul and remembering the Edenic light, warmth, and harmony that once were his.

The progression of meaning is clearly reinforced by the progression of rhythm. The first two lines contain mainly lightly stressed and unstressed syllables, and, although line 1 is in terms of syllables the longest in the poem, it moves along sprightly and quickly: "Myrie it is while sumer ilast." The meter of the line is probably best described as two alternating trochees and iambs with an extra unstressed syllable in the exact center that functions to separate the two parts of the line—more exactly to introduce the second part—and also to prevent the stressed syllables from dominating the line: /X|X/|(X)/X|X/. The alternating trochees and iambs allow unstressed syllables to be grouped together and thus appear dominant. At the same time, the extra unstressed syllable may allow the third foot to be viewed as an amphibrach.

A similar meter is found in the second line—"With fugheles song"—although here the extra unstressed syllable introduces the line: (X)/X|X/. In effect, what we have in these two lines are three verses of alternating trochees and iambs, the second and third of which are introduced by extra syllables that stand for the syntactic expletives *while* and *with*, these being linking words that continue and expand the main thought begun with *Myrie it is*. It is misleading to read these lines as Davies does—"It is pleasant, while summer lasts, with the birds' song" (p. 51)—for the subordinate clause introduced by *while* is neither parenthetical nor preparatory to the prepositional phrase having *with* as its head. Rather, the two structures may be viewed as parallel in showing when and how *it* is *myrie:* "It is merry while summer lasts, [and it is merry] with birds' song [also while this lasts]." The birds' song may be a mark of summer, but summer may likewise be seen in terms of the song, as providing a setting for it. The syntactic difficulties are avoided if we see *Myrie it is* being developed in what follows.

At the same time, if the first line may be said to have initiated a rhythm—the second line, continuing the rhythm, implies that it has— then we might also expect this second line to contain a like number of metrical feet. But in contrast to the tetrameter of line 1, "With fugheles song" may well seem short, metrically deficient, even broken off and incomplete. Indeed, with line 3, introduced by *oc* (but), both thought and rhythm shift to something quite different from what has so far been seen. As winter takes over the thought of the poem, it becomes clear that summer does not *ilast* very long, and *nu*—the stress on this word is not accidental—the good, pleasant times are past. But they were not really at hand when the poem began. Rather, it would seem at this point in the poem that the first two lines were referring to a condition that was more ideal and imagined than actual. The merriment of summer, negated by the present reality, appears to have been only a kind of wistful notion.

The lightly moving lines are replaced in line 3 by a slower, much more heavily accented line: "Oc nu necheth windes blast"—*blast* rhyming with *ilast* but, ironically, referring to that which has prevented the summer from lasting. Line 3 probably begins with an iamb, then becomes trochaic, and ends with an incomplete foot: X/||/X||/X||/. The first two feet exist as the reverse of the rhythm found in the first two lines of the poem. Instead of having trochee play against iamb in that order, the meter is here reversed; and instead of having two unaccented syllables together, two stressed ones stand back to back, creating a sense of heaviness and dramatically negating the previous rhythm. Similarly, the incomplete foot at the end, resulting in the line's having more stresses than nonstresses, adds to the heaviness, as do the plodding iambic dimeter of "And weder strong" (4) and the alliterating /w/ of *windes* (3) and *weder* (4). But line 4 also seems to be cut off. Not only has it fewer syllables than any other line in the poem, it appears to be interrupted or broken into by the *Ei! ei!* cry of the next line.

With line 5 a new metrical element enters the poem. What follows has been prepared for by the shift in tone and mood in lines 3–4, but this next part does not exist in direct relation to the first four lines. Rather, the personal voice of the narrator comes into the poem clearly for the first time, although we should realize that the cry *Ei! ei!*, functioning rhetorically as ecphonesis (*exclamatio*), represents both a contrast to the apparently pleasant *fugheles song* and a development of the *windes blast* that *necheth*—an interesting word that, while literally meaning no more than "draws near," suggests, along with *oc*, the new harshness entering the sound of the poem. *Necheth* is a Scots variant of *neieth*, the word we would expect here and a term that would clearly be seen as onomatopoeic. But even *necheth*—with its medial consonant sound being viewed as the unvoiced dorso-velar fricative [x] instead of the affricate [č]—may be understood both as stating the fact of the wind's approach and as creating its sound. This sound, remarkably like the neighing of a horse, contrasts vividly with the song of the birds and also leads back to the *Ei! ei!* exclamation of the speaker.

The harshness of *Ei! ei!* is continued in the metrical irregularity of line 5, which has no distinct meter at all: "Ei! ei! what this nicht is long." We feel that the discomfort of the long night, and the more regular two lines that follow do not give us consolation: "And ich, wid wel michel wrong, / Soregh and murne and fast." Again the tread is heavy and the movement slow. The /w/ sounds continue, *wid wel*, but are overshadowed by the /r/ of *wrong* (6), which in turn leads to the /r/ of *soregh* and *murne* in the final line. At the same time, the /ŋ/ of the rhyme words *long* and *wrong*, joining the earlier *song* (2) and *strong* (4), appears as the dominant rhyming sound in the poem and provides a further harshness to that permeating this final section.

The last three lines exist generally as a structure of coordination, but within this structure the emphasis shifts from *nicht*, the subject of line 5, to *ich;* and lines 6–7 are in the form of a structure of predication, with the *ich* doing three actions—"soregh and murne and fast"—the statement of which forms the last line. These actions are qualified, however, by the modifying phrase, "wid wel michel wrong," where *wid* most likely means "because of." What is most ambiguous is whether the *wrong* is outside the narrator—is it, say, the cold weather?—or whether it is a state of his own existence, a state for which he is responsible. The very interesting last line makes this second possibility all the more likely. As line 7 is constructed, the three verbs— *soregh, murne, fast*—are linked in a coordinate construction by two *ands*. Our first reaction might well be that these verbs are equivalents, that they are merely three synonyms for the same action, but such is not the case. *Soregh* is the most obvious and expected response to the situation that has been described in the poem, but *murne* implies something else. As sorrowing suggests the response to something immediate, mourning implies the response to something past, to a memory, as it were. It may even be a *recherche du temps perdu* and may refer to the happy times described and created in the first two lines of the poem.

Fast, however, is different from these other verbs, for it implies more than an emotional response to a situation. On a literal level the fasting may be viewed as the necessary response to a condition where food is lacking. But it may also be seen as an act of will, one that functions as an act of penance, even as an act of personal sacrifice, designed to propitiate, as it were, some threatening force. It is, as such, a positive act representing a change from lamentation. It also tends to contrast with the rhyme word *blast* (3), just as that had contrasted with *ilast* (1). In any case, in this final line there seems to be not a paralleling of verbs but a progression from one to the other, from *soregh* to *murne* to *fast*. They all contrast with the first word of the poem, *myrie*; and in this contrast it is possible to see clearly how the tone and mood of the poem have developed and changed.

What is not clear, however, is whether this line represents the final line of the poem. The lower part of the leaf in the manuscript is cut away—even the word *fast* has been supplied by editors—and for all we know—the seven lines here may be but the first stanza of a much longer poem. I myself tend to doubt this possibility and view these lines as a complete and powerful poem. No matter whether there was more to it at one point, what we have now is meaningful and effective as it stands.

Svmer is icumen in—
Lhude sing cuccu!
Groweth sed and bloweth med
4 And springeth the wde nu—
Sing cuccu!

Awe bleteth after lomb,
Lhouth after calue cu;
8 Bulluc sterteth, bucke uerteth—
Murie sing cuccu!
Cuccu, cuccu!
Wel singes thu cuccu—
12 Ne swik thu nauer nu!

Sing cuccu nu, sing cuccu!
Sing cuccu, sing cuccu nu!

Harley MS 978, fol. 11v.
Index, no. 3223, p. 513; *Supplement*, p. 357.

Editions:
  Brown, *13*, no. 6, p. 13.
  Chambers and Sidgwick, no. 2, p. 4.
  Dickins and Wilson, p. 118.
  Davies, no. 3, p. 52.
  Stevick, *One*, no. 3, p. 4.
  Bennett and Smithers, p. 110.

Criticism:
  Wells, p. 491.
  Moore, pp. 50–52.
  Wilson, *Early*, p. 260.
  Schofield, B. "The Provenance and Date of 'Sumer is Icumen in,'" *Music Review*, 9 (1948), 81–86.
  Manning, Stephen, "Sumer Is Icumen In," *Explicator*, 18 (1959), item 2.
  Sikora, *KN*, pp. 236–37.

IN THE FORM of a roundel, or *rota*, this best known of all medieval English lyrics has come down to us as the only English composition in a thirteenth-century commonplace book written by monks of Reading Abbey. It is accompanied in manuscript by Latin instructions for singing, but, even though suggesting that this may be the first English song for six voices, these do not fit the poem very well and probably represent a late addition. Although scholars have argued whether this lyric was essentially a popular composition, based perhaps on Welsh folk song, or whether it was the invention of a learned compos-er,[1] there is no disagreement that the extant poem reveals a great and complex poetic talent.

In its subject it is a *reverdie*, a song of joy in response to the glo-rious coming of spring; and few who know the lyric can help but feel the joy of life it reveals and respond to its exuberance. But the poem has also been subject to some misunderstanding, in part concerning the meaning of the first line, "Svmer is icumen in." The tendency of many modern readers is to view *icumen* as something like "a-coming," making a progressive present tense out of it and thereby suggesting that the transition from winter to summer is taking place at the time of the poem. But *icumen* is clearly a past participle, and, as the line is properly understood, *svmer*, that is spring or warm weather, has al-ready come in; the poet is witnessing and celebrating its presence and its effects on the natural world.

The plants that grow and the young animals that frolic are in fact tangible results, as well as witnesses, of the presence of spring. All of nature is shown to be alive. In lines 3–4—"Groweth sed and bloweth med / And springeth the wde nu"—the verbs describe activity that is taking place at the moment. The coordinate construction in these lines links three occurrences of spring, three evidences of the dynamic and germinating power of *Natura naturans*: the seed grows, the meadow blossoms, and the wood becomes leafy again. Seed, flower, and leaf are linked insofar as they represent three different parts of the world of nature; but the progression from seed to flower to tree also reveals a sense of growth and culmination. Still, even with the /d/ consonance of *sed, med,* and *wde,* these words are not dominant in these two lines. Rather, verbs of action—*groweth, bloweth,* and *springeth*—dominate, revealing the activity of nature alive again after the long winter. This new vitality is the main concern of the poem, as becomes clear in the second stanza when our attention shifts from plant life to animal life.

---

1. See, e.g., Brown, *13*, p. xv, and Moore, p. 51.

The verbs are again the main words: the animals tend to be expressions of all barnyard creatures, and in this sense they are repetitive; our main interest is, rather, in the sounds these animals make. In the first stanza the action described was visual, the growing being an essentially silent action, although we might well imagine the colors of the meadow in bloom (*bloweth med*) and the trees in leaf (*springeth the wde nu*). But in the second stanza, we hear the ewe bleating and the cow lowing (6–7), as both females show their concern for their newly born offspring. Line 8 continues this audial imagery, although here our attention shifts from the mother-child groupings to the adolescent males eager to show their prowess: "Bulluc sterteth, bucke uerteth." The bullock surely refers in this springtime setting to a young, rather than a castrated, bull; and, again in the light of the context, *bucke* is probably to be identified as a he-goat and not as a stag, the former being more appropriate in a barnyard setting.[2] It should be noted, however, that bullock and buck may both be generic terms for young male animals. Still, the poet is not concerned with presenting a catalogue of various springtime sights and sounds. His visions and interests seem to be those of the farmer who looks around his plot of ground and knows that the health of nature contributes to his own well-being.

The dominant sound of the poem is clearly the word *cuccu*, which is uttered ten times in the fourteen lines of the lyric. It may occasionally be a reference to the bird, the cuckoo, as in line 2—"Lhude sing cuccu"—which may be thought of as meaning "Let the cuckoo sing loudly," or even as a direct address to the bird: "Sing loudly, cuckoo!" But it is clearly the sound of *cuccu* that most interests the poet. To *sing cuccu*, that is, to make such a sound, would seem to be to celebrate the glories of spring and to participate in the melodies of nature. Certainly from lines 9–14, including the refrain at the end of the poem, the speaker in his song is continually making the sound *cuccu*. While the cuckoo itself might seem to be out of place in the poem with its barnyard setting, the bird is, nevertheless, appropriate to spring. Being a migratory bird, it was known to arrive in the British Isles in April and was welcomed annually as a harbinger of spring.[3] Also, as may be seen in the writings of St. Hildegard of Bingen, the cuckoo was famous for containing the ingredients essential in the preparation

---

2. There is no need to say, as Moore does, that "in the fourteenth century, as now in isolated regions, the dun deer must have consorted with domesticated bovines" (p. 52).

3. *OED*, 2:1236.

of a remedy for fatigue, and was viewed as a source of rejuvenation.[4]

To say *cuccu* may thus be both to refer to the bird and, because of the echoic nature of its name, to sound like it. Such a line as "Lhude sing Cuccu!" would function as an exclamation and an imperative requesting everyone to join in the melody of life. Through singing *cuccu*, man may be brought into the poem, and symbolically into nature, as he along with everything else celebrates life. The sound *cuccu* may thus be seen possessing a magical quality, as though the repetition of it can bring about a certain desired condition. It is as though the magician's term "Abracadabra!" is what allows his transformations to come about. Here the sound *cuccu* acts both to memorialize and to create the *svmer* that *is icumen in*. More specifically, the final lines of the poem emphasize the continuation of the magical word and also reconstruct the sound of the bird, a sound that is notoriously longlasting. As John Lydgate writes in his redoing of Guillaume Deguileville's *Pèlerinage de la vie humaine*, "I resemble the Cookkoow, / Whych vpon o lay halt so long, / And kan synge noon other song."[5] It is this perpetual sound that comes forth noticeably in the final two lines. These comprise a quasi-refrain and seem to be in response to the imperative "Ne swik thu nauer nu" (12), that is "Do not stop now," or "Never stop." In their repetition the words "Sing cuccu nu, sing cuccu!" become not only dominant but all that exist.

A playful use of *cuccu* may be related to the sound voiced in *uerteth*. Having been mistranslated by several readers—Chambers and Sidgwick for instance translate it as "harbours in the green"[6]—*uerteth*, from OE **feortan*, clearly means "breaks wind." Similarly, the Middle English verb *cukken*, from ON *kuka* (cf. *kakken*) rather than from OF *cuc(c)u*, *cocu*, means "to void excrement."[7] In this light, line 9, "Murie sing cuccu!" may contain a playful continuation of the associations stemming from *uerteth* in the previous line.

Syntactically, the poem is composed of end-stopped lines, most of which are independent clauses or at least complete syntactic units.

---

4. Hildegard of Bingen, *Physica*, vi.viii (*PL* 197:1302). This tradition is the common one in Western European literature and is quite different from that which regards the cuckoo as a bird of sorrow and lamentation, as seen in some medieval Welsh elegies and in the Old English *Seafarer* (53ff.) and *Husband's Message* (23). See the discussion in *The Seafarer*, ed. I. L. Gordon (London, 1960), p. 17.

5. *The Pilgrimage of the Life of Man*, ll.14,382–84, ed. F. J. Furnivall, EETS ES 83 (London, 1901), pp. 388–89.

6. P. 4.

7. *MED*, 2:782.

Only lines 3–4 tend to be joined to form one thought, but even here the construction is coordinate, with the parts being linked by the two *ands*.[8] Moreover, as Sikora states, the lines show great simplicity in their grammatical structure. Not only are they in the form of simple sentences, they seem to be constructed in terms of one basic pattern which, notwithstanding the ambiguity of *cuccu*, may be formulated as subject-verb-(adverb).[9] The adverb is optional, at times, as in line 3, being omitted; and at other times, as in line 2, the order of the grammatical elements varies. In terms of overall movement, the poem begins with the statement of its subject (1) and the view the audience should have of this subject (2), then moves to a series of particularizations about the results of *svmer*'s existence and, as it were, the effects of the sound *cuccu*. The two kinds of particularizations, vegetable and animal, are punctuated and separated by the everpresent *sing cuccu*.

Within most lines is a noticeable assonance (for instance, /uw/ in line 2) or consonance (/l/ in 6), giving the impression that each line is marked by a key sound, although sometimes the sound is actually a combination of vowel and consonant (/um/ in 1). The third line in each stanza of the poem proper is marked by a double assonance and an internal rhyme: "Groweth sed and bloweth med" (4) and "Bulluc sterteth, bucke uerteth" (8). The impression is that these lines could be cut in two. Moreover, these two stanzas are joined together by means of several sounds and words: *lhude*, the first word of line 2, is echoed by *lhouth* (7), likewise the first word in the second line of the stanza; and *nu* (4) at the end of stanza 1 is repeated at the end of stanza 2 (12).

But it is, of course, the repetition of *cuccu* that holds everything together and that acts as the dominant element in the poem. The sound may have partially dictated the syntax of line 7, "Lhouth after calue cu." Both the line before and the line after it reveal normal word order, but here the inversion seems designed to allow the word *cu* to be in a rhymed and dominant position. Still, the success of this lyric is due not only to the manipulating of the sound and the suggestion of *cuccu*, but to the concise and subtle patterning of various sounds and actions whereby the developing exuberance catches up and embraces the listener.

---

8. Sikora points out that, according to the musical notation, terminal junctures occur after lines 2, 4, 5, 7, 9, and 12 (p. 236).

9. Sikora, *KN*, p. 237.

Nou goth sonne vnder wod:
Me reweth, Marie, thi faire rode.
Nou goth sonne vnder tre:
Me reweth, Marie, thi sone and the.

Bodl. MS 21599, formerly Arch. Selden, supra 74 (3462), fol. 55v.
Index, no. 2320, p. 365; *Supplement*, p. 270.

Editions:
> Brown, *13*, no. 1, p. 1.
> Davies, no. 6, p. 54.
> Stevick, *One*, no. 4, p. 5.
> Bennett and Smithers, p. 129.

Criticism:
> Cutler, John L., "Nou Goth Sonne Vnder Wod," *Explicator*, 4 (1945), item 7.
> Kane, p. 140.
> Thayer, C. G., "Nou Goth Sonne Under Wod," *Explicator*, 11 (1953), item 25.
> Manning, Stephen, "Nou goth Sonne vnder wod," *MLN*, 74 (1959), 578–81;
>   reproduced with minor changes in *Wisdom*, pp. 80–83.
> Lockwood, W.B. "A Note on the Middle English 'Sunset on Calvary,'" *ZAA*,
>   9 (1961), 410–12.
> Stevick, *MP*, p. 115.
> Reiss, *CE*, 27 (1966), 375–76.
> Dronke, *ML*, pp. 64–65.

FOUND IN AN EARLY THIRTEENTH-CENTURY French text of Archbishop Edmund Riche's *Speculum Ecclesie*—as well as in at least forty-one additional manuscripts of the *Speculum*—these lines, said to have been written by *un Engleis*, follow a reference to Canticles 1:6 "Look not upon me for I am black, because the sun has looked upon me." Although it has been suggested that the lines might be the initial ones of a longer poem, there is no need to view them as such. They form a self-contained unit and make an effective piece of poetry.

The dominant method of the lyric is to use imagery that plays on the related double meanings of certain words. Through this imagery the poem comments on the crucifixion and provides a celebration of the Virgin Mary. The words *son(n)e, wod, rode,* and *tre,* all ambiguous, are all key words. From what would seem to be in the first line an innocent, though perhaps euphemistic, description of a sunset,[1] with the sun going down behind the trees, the tone changes in the second line to give a sense of foreboding: "Me reweth, Marie, thi faire rode." With *reweth,* the strongest word both in the line and, as it is repeated later, in the whole poem, we may wonder what Mary's countenance, *rode,* has to do with the sunset. Our first thought may be that the setting sun has perhaps struck the Virgin's face at such an angle and with such a color of light that the face contains something which the narrator finds strange. But then in the last two lines we understand that, like the sun in the sky, Mary's son is also going under, as it were, on *his* tree—a parallel existing whether or not *sonne* and *sone* are homophonic, for the sun was supposed to have grown dark at the moment of Christ's death[2]—and at this point we may realize that *rode* (2) contains the meaning of "cross."

Wod (1), *rode* (2), and *tre* (3) are all suggestive of the cross and thereby the crucifixion, without in any instance the poet's stating denotatively the specific subject of his poem. This indirect approach is effective in that it allows the crucifixion to be the background of the poem while the foreground is concerned with the narrator's compassion for Mary at the foot of the cross. But even this pity is not the main theme being brought out in this lyric. The poem begins as an apparent description of nature, then changes to a lament for Mary, a reflection on her grief, and finally becomes a realization of suffering and of the coming of night and death to the world. Sunset and the death of Christ are made to parallel and give further implications to each other.

---

1. Lockwood, pp. 410–12.

2. On this point, Dronke cites a verse by Walter of Châtillon: "Sol eclypsium patitur / dum sol verus moritur" (*ML*, p. 64).

The power and suggestiveness of these few lines may be seen further by attempting to translate them into modern English. In one recent rendering they appear as follows:

> Now sinks the sun beneath the wood
> (Mary, I pity your lovely face);
> Now sinks the sun beneath the Rood
> (Mary, I pity your Son and you).[3]

The translation has reduced and altered the Middle English original, limiting its suggestiveness, changing its tone, and causing the integral connection between the two subjects, the crucifixion and Mary, to be lost. In this modernization lines 2 and 4 are subordinated to the thoughts of lines 1 and 3, and act as a refrain of sorts. The original, on the other hand, uses something like reverse ballad meter, with what I view as a trimeter line preceding a tetrameter one. Lines 1 and 3, the action of the crucifixion, are, in any case, short and, as it were, final; lines 2 and 4, longer and more drawn out, are reflective. The action of the crucifixion is at each point commented on indirectly by the narrator, who focuses on Mary rather than on the death of Christ. His response is interwoven into the preceding action, giving the impression of a subordinated or hypotactic structure, although the poem is really paratactic, with each line representing a separate independent clause.

Even though lines 1, 3 and 2, 4 clearly parallel each other, the overall division in the structure is after line 2. Here is the main juncture of the poem, separating the initial end-stopped couplet from the final one. But as Stevick points out, the lines are syntactically in the form of four one-line sentences; and in neither couplet is one line explicitly subordinated to the other or explicitly coordinated.[4] Still, the couplet division is functional in that line 2 depends for its effect on line 1, and line 1 is given expanded and deeper meaning through line 2. Together as a unit they lead to the last couplet where the process is repeated. This final two-line unit, however, both gives additional meaning to each of the lines comprising it and also expands the sense of the first couplet—just as the final phrase of the second,

---

3. *Medieval English Verse,* trans. Brian Stone (Baltimore, 1964), p. 36.

4. Stevick, *MP,* p. 115; commenting on this structure, he adds, "It is just this implicit structuring of the expression, keeping in this instance the maximum correlation between line and unit of complete utterance, that elicits the psychological, temporal, doctrinal, and other connections the reader can supply and sets the mode within which these connections are to be made."

"thi sone and the" (4), expands the equivalent phrase of the first, "thi faire rode" (2).

The first word of each couplet, *nou*, serves further to link the two parts of the poem together. Repeated in line 3, it not only suggests the restatement to come in the second couplet but gives the impression that even though the action referred to is the same in each couplet, it is taking place at two different times. That is, the first *nou* may not be the same moment as the second; some time may have passed between the events referred to in the couplets. What is created is the sense of a movement to darkness and death. With this movement goes a developing complexity and a sense of paradox and ambiguity, brought about through paranomasia, where secular words come to have religious significance, and through incremental repetition, where innocuous terms become suggestive. When "Nou goth sonne vnder wod" (1) changes to "Nou goth sonne vnder tre" (3), a general, collective word is replaced by a particular, concrete—and more symbolic —term. The repetition of *sonne* here also leads to the expanded and intensified sun-son wordplay seen in the final line.

The narrator's sorrow is apparently likewise intensified as the light grows dimmer and as darkness comes to the world, and the poem concludes on a note of real grief—the second *reweth* is much stronger than the first—as the narrator feels the sadness and loss. While the poem describes the crucifixion, it does so in such an oblique way that even though the narrator appears as a witness, he would seem to be a witness not to any imminent resurrection but to the darkness that has come with the death of Christ. If, however, we are to understand this poem in terms of the Canticles reference that preceded it in manuscript, we should realize that the darkness is really the way to light and that the poem suggests the movement from sin to redemption. The compassion felt by the narrator may be seen as the first step to contrition, which is the way to repentance and salvation.

Although this lyric has a freshness unusual in the many medieval poems on the subject of the crucifixion, we should not be deceived into thinking that its wordplay and ambiguities are present merely to give intellectual pleasure. Rather, functioning to reveal unexpected depths of meaning, they lead to an awareness of a moral or tropological significance and perhaps to a new way of life—in this particular piece to something that would give concrete shape to the state of mind revealed by *reweth*. The narrator functions as our guide to the scene re-created before our eyes, and his words, showing us the proper response, indirectly ask us to participate in the grieving and to recognize anew the whole meaning of the crucifixion.

Foweles in the frith,
The fisses in the flod,
And i mon waxe wod.
4   Mulch sorw I walke with
For beste of bon and blod.

Bodl. MS 21713, formerly Douce 139, fol. 5.
Index, no. 864, p. 138; *Supplement*, p. 102.

Editions:
   Brown, *13*, no. 8, p. 14.
   Chambers and Sidgwick, no. 3, p. 5.
   Davies, no. 4, p. 52.
   Stevick, *One*, no. 17, p. 25.
   Dickins and Wilson, p. 119.
   Bennett and Smithers, p. 111.

Criticism:
   Moore, p. 29.
   Sikora, *KN*, pp. 233–36.
   Reiss, *CE*, 27 (1966), 376–77.
   Jeremy, Sister Mary, "*Mon* in 'Foweles in the Frith,'" *ELN*, 5 (1967), 80–81.
   Luisi, David, "'Foweles in the Frith,'" *Explicator*, 25 (1967), item 47.
   Manning, *CL*, pp. 239–40.

THIS LYRIC is in some ways similar to "Nou goth sonne vnder wod," although the particular thought that acts as the basis or occasion for this poem is not so explicit as it was in the other, and although the sorrow of the narrator seems here less formal and more personal than in the previous poem. While "Foweles in the frith"—apparently a two-part song—may be similar in tone to a complaint poem in the courtly love tradition,[1] the nature of the narrator's sorrow is ambiguous; and as I read the poem, it is every bit as religious as the preceding lyric. In its expression of human isolation, it may even be recognized as a paraphrase in personal terms of the familiar passage in Matthew 8:20 and Luke 9:58: "Foxes have their holes, birds their roosts; but the Son of Man has nowhere to lay his head."

This poem also contains verbal ambiguities as revelant and meaningful as those in the earlier lyric. For instance *wod* (3) continues in a sense the places represented by *frith* (forest) and *flod* (sea) of the two preceding lines—functioning in one respect like the *wod* in line 1 of "Nou goth sonne vnder wod." It thus acts in a series—*frith, flod, wod*—that parallels the other series, *foweles, fisses,* and *i.* But at the same time, in its most applicable meaning here of "mad," *wod* serves to distinguish and separate man from the rest of nature. The fowls and fish are content in their environment, but man is deranged and out of harmony with the world around him. While *wod* as "wood" and *wod* as "mad" are not phonologically exact, a play on words may still be possible, at least in the context of this particular poem.

The last two lines give meaning to and expand the idea of isolation suggested in the first three lines. Although man may seem to be initially joined with the other living beings, he is really different from them: they fly above and swim beneath the surface of the earth, but he is limited to its surface. He walks and, furthermore, walks alone with *mulch sorw* (4), while the fowls and fish apparently are with others of their own kind. The /w/ sounds in lines 3 and 4 tend to join *walke* with *waxe wod* and suggest that these two actions of man are related. *Waxe* also serves to link the growth of the narrative *I* to that of the fowls and fish and, again, to contrast with their growth; for the narrator grows *wod*, mad.

Nor is madness to be regarded as merely a temporary state in the narrator's life; it is, on the other hand, the result of man's living after original sin. To be a beast (*beste,* 5) of bone and blood means, as it

---

1. Most recently stated by Manning, *CL*, pp. 239–40. Sikora also questions its classification as an "amorous poem" and feels that religious elements exist at least implicitly in it (p. 236).

were, to experience *mulch sorw* (4). Also, at least insofar as its ortho-graphy indicates, *beste* may signify "best," a meaning that shows the term to be doubly ironic. To be the "best" of bone and blood, to be man, is paradoxically to *waxe wod* and to be the most sorrowful of creatures.[2] The separation of man from the rest of nature implied here is like that seen in Alan of Lille's *Complaint of Nature*, where Nature's garb is shown to be rent by man's actions, an idea going back to the description of Philosophy in Boethius' *Consolation of Philosophy*. A further implication here may be that the narrator, like a scapegoat, carries on his shoulders the weight of human sin and its resultant sorrow. Along with being fallen man, he also approximates Christ as man of sorrows. Indeed, *beste* as "best" may be a more pointed ref-erence to Christ, to him who was the best of living beings. Because of Christ and his suffering, the narrator sorrows; also, because of Christ, he has additional responsibility in that he now knows his obli-gations and the need for redemption. Not to stretch the point too much, the predicament of the narrator here is like that Sartre says is the human condition, when responsible man feels the anguish, for-lornness, and despair of being alive. If the narrator were one of the "foweles in the frith" or one of the "fisses in the flod," such problems would not be his.

It is difficult to accept the view stated by Moore that the poem is unsuccessful because the nature setting is "insufficiently articulated with the poet's love-longing."[3] While I am perfectly willing to say that love-longing may be a partial cause of the narrator's grief, the poem is certainly talking about more than this. To make love-longing, which is not even clearly present, the main theme, as well as the basis for judging the success of the poem, is clearly to mishandle the work. While recognizing that much of the power of this piece is due to its understatement—that is, the author does not work out a moral or give us anything explicitly didactic—we should also realize the nature and effectiveness of its verbal ambiguities. "Nou goth sonne vnder wod" centered on the ambiguities of a few words; this poem, on the other hand, primarily uses contrasting elements to make its point. With the exception of *beste* with its two possible meanings, this lyric tends to use patterns of words that create meaning through their relationships to each other.

---

2. Although it is unlikely, if the auxiliary *mon*—primarily meaning "must"—may be seen as the noun "man" and in apposition with *i*, such a connection would be even more meaningful. This meaning is suggested by Jeremy, pp. 80–81.

3. Moore, p. 29.

The syntactic ambiguity of the first three lines is a good example of the way these word-patterns function to give developed and heightened meaning: "Foweles in the frith, / The fisses in the flod, / And i mon waxe wod." At first we do not know whether the three lines represent three independent clauses in paratactic structure—with the verbs of the first two lines missing but understood as forms of "to be"—or whether *foweles, fisses,* and *i* are all to be seen as plural and parallel subjects of the verb *mon waxe* (must grow, 3)— though *mon* is properly a singular auxiliary. When we understand that the first structure, based on an elliptical copula, is the more likely and the more operative —even though it is a type of ellipsis not frequently found in Middle English syntax[4]—we also realize that the linking verbs, implied in the first two lines, do not need to be stated. The state of being of the *foweles* and *fisses* is clear enough, especially since the prepositional phrase following each of these substantives serves to modify and ground them. They are permanent in their setting; but man has no setting— he exists only through a verb of action.

Although all the lines in the poem consist of six syllables, the rhythms vary and are worth noting. Lines 1 and 2 have two major stresses each, but then in line 3—the key line of the poem—the rhythm changes. As I read it, *i, mon, waxe,* and *wod* should all be stressed, the basic two-stressed meter of the first two lines thus being replaced by this essentially spondaic line with four stresses. Line 4 again contains two primary stresses—"Mulch sórw I wálke with"—but the line is different from 1 and 2, as the narrator is different from the fowls and fish. This difference is marked principally by the feminine ending *walke with:* after stressed *walke* appears an unaccented syllable, giving the impression that the line is stumbling, and thereby reflecting the state of the narrator's mind. The final line—"For beste of bon and blod"—contains three major stresses and, although regularly iambic, continues the sorrow through the /b/ alliteration of the stressed words *beste, bon,* and *blod.*

In its rhyme scheme the poem appears to be constructed in terms of a quatrain, *abab,* with an additional *b* rhyme after line 2. This key line (3) not only alters the existing rhythm, it also changes the emphasis from what is outside man to the narrator himself. And the line is noticeably personal, contrasting with the rather detached and innocuous remarks of lines 1–2. The emphasis on man and his personal feelings continues in line 4; but then in the final line the direction seems to turn again to the creatures other than man although, with

---

4. Sikora, *KN,* p. 234.

beste being ambiguous, it may still be a reference to man, whose problem is clearly at the heart of this poem.[5]

Ending on a note of bewilderment and deep melancholy, the poem is as close as the medieval lyric would seem to be able to get to giving a personal response to the inadequacies of man's existence and to the spiritual burdens put on him by Christianity. If man were carefree, he could be as innocent as the fowls, fish, and the rest of nature. But, special creature that he is, man knows that his life has a spiritual purpose and point. This knowledge would seem, ironically, to make him further *waxe wod* and to drive him to greater *sorw*, which, as it increases, makes him become like the melancholy man who has no faith, hope, or charity, and who is spiritually dead. The line between concern and despair, the unforgiveable sin, is a fine one, and few can walk it unscathed.

---

5. Luisi points out that "the dichotomy between thoughts of the first two lines wherein the poet's gaze is turned outward, and those of the last three, wherein he scrutinizes his own inner state, rests upon the poet's recognition of the tension between what is as it *should be* (the natural order of the universe) and what is as it *ought not to be* (the human capacity to oppose that order)."

Naueth my saule bute fur and ys,
　　And the lichome eorthe and treo:
　　Bidde we alle then heye kyng
4　　That welde schal the laste dom,
　　That he vs lete that ilke thing,
　　　That we mowen his wille don;
　　He vs skere of the tything
8　　That sunfule schulle an-vnderfon,
　　Hwenne deth heom lat to the murehthe
　　　That neuer ne byth undon.
　　　　Amen.

Jesus College, Oxford, MS 29, Pt. 2, fol. 189.
Supplement, *2284.5, p. 264 (see *Index*, Acephalous Poem *44,
　　p. 695).

Editions:
　　Old English Miscellaney, ed. Richard Morris, EETS OS 49 (London, 1872),
　　　pp. 100–01.
　　Stevick, *One*, no. 20, p. 33.

Criticism:
　　Reiss, *Style*, pp. 97–102.

THIS PRAYER asking God to hold back Judgment Day so that the narrator may repent has been strangely neglected. Not in any of the standard collections, it has, however, been anthologized by Stevick and hopefully will be better known than it has been. Its theme is certainly familiar, if not overly familiar, and may remind readers of English poetry of John Donne's famous sonnet on the subject. Similarly, its first lines may call up Robert Frost's ironic little poem on the world's ending in fire and ice. But the virtues of this thirteenth-century lyric are real, and it does not need to rely on creating a response through the pleasant associations it may call up in the minds of its audience.

The first two lines act as a setting for the prayer that occupies the next eight lines, but they are more than a prelude or introduction to what is to come. In them the helplessness of man is revealed but stated in such a way as to be ambiguous and compelling. We are forced to pause and understand just what and how much is being said here. It is puzzling to learn that the soul has only fire and ice and the body only earth and wood—*naueth . . . but*, meaning "has nothing but," is the operative predicate in each of the first two lines of the poem. The poet is not saying what soul and body are but what they have, that is, what they possess, or, more likely, what their end will be. There may well be an "ashes to ashes" suggestion here, but the more pertinent meaning seems to be that the body can most likely anticipate only the wood of the coffin and the earth in which it will lie, while the soul similarly will have for its end or resting place the fire and ice that in the medieval view characterized hell.[1] As *eorthe and treo* (2) are essentially the same, so are *fur and ys* (1). Moreover, the two pairs are related in that they mark the end of the entity that "has" these things. The opening lines may thus be viewed as giving a personal statement of despair, where the narrator of the poem realizes what is likely in store for him inasmuch as he is a sinful mortal, and what is in store for all who are like him.

The necessity for repentance is real, and we are willing to join the narrator who asks us all to pray to God. There is a change of pace from the individual (*my*, 1) to mankind in general (*we alle*, 3), who appear as the subjects of the *heye kyng* (3) who will *welde*, that is, rule over, the Last Judgment (*laste dom*, 4). But *welde* also suggests

---

1. See, e.g., Dante's conception of Hell and the fresco by Nardi di Cioni, in Robert Hughes, *Heaven and Hell in Western Art* (New York, 1968), p. 158. See also the descriptions of hell in medieval vision literature, such as the Vision of Tundale and St. Patrick's Purgatory, and the references in Howard R. Patch, *The Other World, According to Descriptions in Medieval Literature* (Cambridge, 1950), pp. 111, 129.

that it is a club that God is wielding, one that he will use to hurl body and soul to their destruction, referred to here cautiously and indirectly as *that ilke thing* (5), as well as euphemistically as *the tything* (7) and *the murehthe* (mirth, 9). The last two lines offer another change of person: after referring to the *sunfule* (8), the narrator shifts his pronominal reference to *heom* (them, 9). These are the ones who will be taken away by death, and the narrator disassociates himself from them.

The division between the initial personal statement and the subsequent prayer is marked by a shift in the number of stresses in line 2. Except for this line and line 10, the last one in the poem, both of which are in trimeter, the usual number of stresses per line is four. The reduction of stresses in these two lines may imply the finishing of a thought and a sense of finality. Such is the impression even though, interestingly, neither line 2 nor 10 rhymes with the line immediately preceding it. But the resulting unrhymed alternating tetrameter and trimeter gives a framework to the central tetrameter sestet, which forms the bulk of the prayer. This section (3–8), in alternating rhyme, creates a drawn-out structure of subordination, each part of which after the first line (3) is introduced by the relative pronoun *that*—even line 7 is implicitly introduced by *that*. This structure both keeps the prayer going and creates a series of parallel clauses that refer back to line 3 and that lead to the concluding two lines, which, while also employing a *that* clause (10), turn away from the prayer that God delay Judgment Day to a statement of what will be the fate of sinners. This statement in turn leads back to the first two lines, where the ultimate fate of the narrator is predicted.

The construction of this central prayer is rather intricate and deserves comment. It begins with an independent clause in the subjunctive or imperative mood—"Bidde we alle then heye kyng"—the first words of this prayer meaning something like "let us pray (to)." What follows in the next lines refers back to or modifies various elements in this utterance. In line 4, "That welde schal the laste dom," *that* introduces an adjectival clause modifying *kyng* and making meaningful the descriptive adjective *heye* (3). In referring explicitly to *the laste dom*, line 4 also gives a reference point for understanding the significance of both the prayer and the fear, expressed in the first two lines, that was its cause. Conversely, in line 5—"That he vs lete that ilke thing"— *that* introduces a noun clause which functions as direct object of *bidde* (4). It begins the statement, contained in the following lines, of what is being asked of God.

This is the main point of the poem, that God "vs lete that ilke thing," with *thing* taking its meaning from the reference to the final judgment in the previous line. But the statement is rather ambiguous in that *lete* here means not "allow" but something like "delay" or "keep from." The narrator is certainly not asking for Doomsday but wishing rather that God keep it from man or protect mankind from it. In the next line, "That we mowen his wille don" (6), *that* means "so that" and introduces an adverbial clause which continues this thought. The narrator wants God not to will Judgment Day yet so that man will have time to do God's will.

Lines 7–8 represent a restatement of 5–6, though stating the thought in more explicit terms: "He vs skere of the tything / That sunfule schulle an-vnderfon." Although line 7 begins without a *that*, one is in effect present in that the line likewise refers back to *bidde* (3) and acts, along with line 5, as its direct object. The parallelism with lines 5–6 is also clear even though 7–8 are in the form of noun clause and adjective clause. In the earlier lines the request was that God would *vs lete* (5); here it is that he will *vs skere*, that is, free or excuse us from the Judgment which, continuing the euphemism, is referred to innocuously as a *tything*, ostensibly a tithe, something owed by man to God, but also perhaps signifying "wages" or even "reward." Since it is a *tything* that the sinful will receive (8), the term is obviously ironic. Such bitter humor and irony tend to increase in the final lines, culminating in the description of the pains of hell as *murehthe* (mirth, 9). A parallelism similar to *vs lete* and *vs skere* may be found in *that ilke thing* (5) and *the tything* (7), especially if the latter phrase is read as *that tything. That* instead of *the* would both reinforce the parallelism of the phrase and be justifiable for metrical reasons in that, as the line stands, *the* must receive a stress—a kind of awkwardness not found elsewhere in this poem. Moreover, the poet has been directing our attention to something particular, something best expressed as *that;* and the two uses of adjectival *that* would play nicely against the two instances of relative *that* introducing the subordinate clauses (6, 8).

In any case, the last two lines, in the form of an adverbial followed by an adjectival clause, represent the culmination of the two noun clauses as they reexpress what is feared about *the laste dom* (5): "Hwenne deth heom lat to the murehthe / That neuer ne byth un-don" (9–10). The Dance of Death may seem to be a merriment, but for those who are led away it is only horror. There may even be a wordplay in *murehthe*, for its spelling is strange. While meaning "mirth," it may also suggest a state of "mirk" or a darkness that is without end. It is "mirth" also in the sense that perhaps too much of a concern for the pleasures of this world is what causes one to be led to this final punishment which may resemble, by being in accord with, the sin that created it.

Another instance of wordplay may be found in *lat* (9). Correctly read by Stevick as a contracted present form of *leodeth*, it is unfortunately expanded to this form in his edition,[2] causing, consequently, any possible wordplay between *lat* and *lete* (5) to be lost. As opposed to the contrite and penitent who hopefully will have their Judgment Day *lete* or held back, the sinful will be led forth (*lat*) to their eternal agony. In like manner, the last word of line 10, *undon*, describes both the eternality of this punishment and what has happened to these sinners—they have been undone. It may thus contrast with *don* (6), which refers to the accomplishment of the contrite in serving God and acting well. To *don* God's will is to avoid being *undon*. It is also to change before there will be no change.

The poem is finally an assertion of man's inherent helplessness, along with his need to follow the *heye kyng* (3) and have God as his protector. Only then is there any hope for man. The narrator knows what he must do, and the poem itself acts as a means of doing it. In this lyric we see his frustration and concern; in that he is enlightened, he acts as a spokesman for mankind, whom he asks to join him in his prayer, which is in the form of an elaborate single sentence. At the end of the sentence is death or salvation, but at this point, while the sentence is still in process, the choice for the outcome seems to be man's. We get the impression that if he acts as he should, what follows will represent a happy ending; if he does not, there is only disintegration for his body and *fur and ys* for his soul.

---

2. Stevick, *One*, p. 33.

Quanne hic se on rode
Ihesu, mi lemman,
An besiden him stonden
4 Marie an Iohan;
And his rig isuongen,
And his side istungen,
For the luue of man:
8 Wel ou hic to wepen
And sinnes forleten,
Yif hic of luue kan,
Yif hic of luue kan,
12 Yif hic of luue kan.

Royal MS 12.E.1., fol. 194v.
Index, no. 3964, p. 635; *Supplement,* p. 455.

Editions:
Brown, *13,* no. 35B, pp. 62–63.
Davies, no. 30, p. 99.
Stevick, *One,* no. 14B, p. 22.

Criticism:
Manning, *Wisdom,* p. 142.
Oliver, p. 99.

ON A SUBJECT very popular in medieval lyrical poetry, this poem is related to at least three other extant short pieces all beginning "When I see on rood." The others, however, are markedly inferior to this one both metrically and in terms of the development of the thought from beginning to end. In the form of a single sentence representing a developed "when-then" construction, this poem tends to deceive in its casualness. Beginning as an informal report of sorts, it gives the impression that the speaker is stating a condition of habit or a fact of existence, something like, "When I see the leaves fall, I know that autumn is here." But the "When I see" here is of no such prosaic matter. Jesus on the cross represents a condition at the center of life for Christian man. The crucifixion itself is the nadir of human existence, as the concomitant resurrection is its zenith.

The first two lines not only call up the crucifixion; they also ask us to see it with the narrator as though it is happening at the moment of the poem. The image, moreover, seems to be of the actual crucifixion, not an artistic representation of it. This event is re-created, as it were, and occurring at the time of the poem's composition. The narrator does not say, "When I *saw* Jesus on the cross." The present tense *se* (1) demands our attention and fixes it to the immediacy of the scene. The resultant effect is of something strange. We may rationalize and say that the speaker is referring to the many standardized representations of the crucifixion that would permeate his daily life, but it is clearly—as the developing poem makes meaningful—the sight of the crucified Christ himself that causes the speaker to respond as he does. And the "when" clause focuses on the particulars of the scene. Alongside Christ in the foreground are Mary and John, acting as our entry into the poem, serving, as it were, to make the event public. Also, Christ's suffering is described: his back is scourged (*isuongen*, 5) and his side is pierced (*istungen*, 6). These are harsh sights and harsh words, which in their emphasis create a feeling of the agony and horror. In leading to the assertion that this suffering is "for the luue of man" (7), they also tend to function ironically.

Our response to this scene and to its immediacy is then questioned in the last part of the poem (8–12), which comprises the "then" clause. In this section the narrator no longer tells us what he feels but rather what, because of the crucifixion, he *should* feel and do: "Wel ou hic to wepen" (8). He certainly ought to weep and, furthermore, to convert his feelings into actions. He should obviously repent (*forleten*, 9) of his sins. But the ending is primarily on a note of the conditional: the narrator does not tell us either what he does or what explicitly we should do. We get the final impression, reinforced by the repetition of "Yif hic of luue kan," that he knows what he should do but feels the frustration of not being able to do it—at least not so much as he should and not so much as he needs to. The poem thus acts as a cry of despair, a feeling of frustration that the crucifixion is being wasted, and that man is not being saved. The narrator speaks not just for himself as an individual man with a unique problem, but also for men who, aware of the crucifixion and of Christ's love for them, have not in turn shown love to him. In effect, the narrator questions that human love which cannot respond significantly to Christ's love, a question that involves man's comprehension of Christian love and his actual ability to love. The frustration of seeing, understanding, responding with feeling, and then not acting on the basis of the new insight is driven home by the repetition of the statement about knowing love (10–12).

The development of this lyric resembles in its asymmetry that of a Petrarchan sonnet. Here corresponding to the Petrarchan octave are the first seven lines of the poem and to the sestet the last five lines. The rhyme scheme is rather complex, with rhyme becoming a noticeable feature only by the end of the first section (5–6). The first line, in fact, stands alone in the poem, acting in its unrhymed independence as a separate preliminary element, a starting point, as it were, for what follows. Our initial reaction to this first line—"Quanne hic se on rode" —might be that it is corrupt, that it lacks a word at its end that would rhyme with *stonden* (3), for instance. But a comparison of this lyric to the other versions indicates that word and line exist elsewhere (Brown, number 34) without rhyme. In the version closest to this one (Brown, number 35A) the first line has *idon* following *rode* ("Wenne hic soe on rode idon");[1] but this provides what is at best an inexact rhyme with the *an* endings of later lines. In Brown, number 37, *rode*, likewise the last word in the first line, rhymes with *stode* ("Qvanne I zenke onne þe rode / quorupe-one þu stode"). But this *stode* is not, as one might at first think, a substitute so as to get rid of *stonden*: this word appears in number 37 as *stondende*, the rhyme word two lines later. What seems most likely is that the first line represents a standard phrase that has meaning and power of its own. Even though it partially rhymes with line 3 through the assonance of /ɔ/, it really functions outside the sound patterns of what follows, and is preliminary to the sense of the rest of the poem.

Following this unrhymed line, lines 2, 4, and 7 rhyme in terms of /an/; and lines 3, 5, and 6 are linked by a somewhat less precise sound

---

1. For a view of this version, see Woolf, pp. 33–34.

pattern of /ɔn-en/. But the dominant phoneme, occurring in all but the initial line, is a nasal or, more precisely, a profusion of nasals, mainly /n/, revealed most consistently in the unstressed endings of the lines. Along with this pervasive nasal goes an assonance generally centering on the mid back vowel /ɔ/, as in *stonden* (3) and, though less precisely, in *rode* (1) and *Iohan* (4). This vowel sound tends to develop to a high back vowel /u/ in *isuongen* (5) and *istungen* (6), becoming finally the dominant vocalic, in the dominant word *luue*, in lines 7 and 10–12. Throughout the poem the progression, as seen in almost every line, is from a stressed front vowel to a stressed back vowel. The front vowel is either /ey/, as in *se* (1) and *Ihesu* (2), or /iy/, as in *besiden* (3) and *side* (6)—*rig* (5) and *sinnes* (9) represent an /i/ variant. Most pronounced within the "when" clause, the front vowels in the first stressed syllable move to /o/, /ɔ/, and /u/ back vowels in the second stress—for instance, *hic* to *rode* (1). Line 7, on the other hand, shows the reverse of this phonemic pattern: "For the luue of man." Here, in what is the last line of the "when" clause, the pattern of stress is from the back vowel /u/ to the central vowel /a/, producing a reversal that tends to isolate the line and make it stand out from what has preceded it. Such an effect is aided by a shift in the stress pattern, from the feminine endings of lines 1–6 to the masculine one of line 7. This emphasis is indeed appropriate, for the line is a key one in the poem.

The first seven lines, the septet, should also be seen as subdivided into two parts, lines 1–4 representing in terms of meter a quatrain with two stresses per line. The stress pattern may be best described as amphibrachic, X/X|X/X—as in "Quanne hic se on rode" (1)—even though line 3 begins with an extra unstressed syllable and though line 2 is in the form of a trochee followed by an amphibrach. Line 4, depending on how *Marie* is stressed, is like either line 1 or line 2. With line 5, however, the first line after the initial quatrain, the rhythm tends to shift to what is clearly an anapest plus amphibrach construction, XX/|X/X—"And his rig isuongen"—which continues to line 7, "For the luue of man." This line then, for purposes of emphasis, drops the feminine ending necessary to the amphibrach and concludes with an iamb that, with its terminal juncture, makes the line appear shorter and less metrically regular than the preceding lines, though such is not the case at all. It is perhaps as an afterthought that we realize that *luue of man* (7) represents an expansion of *lemman* (2). The key word *luue* is thus tied to an earlier term. In line 2 Jesus was seen as *mi lemman;* here the direction has changed and it is Jesus who now shows the love.

The second part of the poem, the "then" clause, begins as did the first part with lines of two amphibrachic feet—"Wel ou hic to wepen / And sinnes forleten" (8–9)—that comprise a couplet rhyming through homoeoteleuton on the vocalic /ey/. Line 10, "Yif hic of luue kan," provides, however, another break in the rhythm, but one that has been influenced by that of the preceding couplet. In the form of iamb followed by anapest, X/|XX/, line 10 shows the reverse of the rhythm of line 7, the climaxing line of the "when" clause. But line 10 is not the final line of the poem, even though it is in some other versions of the lyric that are without repetition.

While we cannot know exactly how the stress patterns change as this line is twice repeated, we may profitably examine some of the possibilities. I have found that at first reading most people view line 10 as having the metrical pattern suggested above—iamb plus anapest —then look at line 11 as though with some surprise and stress it somewhat tentatively, keeping the primary accent on the *hic* but using what are at best secondary or half stresses for *luue* and *kan*—a reading that tends to emphasize *hic* and, by trailing off in unaccented and half-accented syllables, to suggest hesitation and indecision. When these readers come to line 12, they then reverse the procedure and over-emphasize where they had formerly understated, so that the final line reads like this: X/|X//. And in some instances the first word *Yif* receives tertiary or even secondary stress. The result of such a reading is to reaffirm the reading of line 10, which in the process of development was briefly doubted in line 11. If this reading of the last three lines may be seen as likely for the speaker of the poem, the reaffirmation in line 12 may suggest his intention to remedy the frustrating situation and act as it, as well as his emotional response to it, demands. But the reaffirmation also functions to persuade the audience of the poem that they too should take decisive action. The final emotion of the lyric may then be called one of determination. There is no victory as such but a realization of inadequacy and a fervent desire to do something about it.[2]

The syntactic shape of this poem is largely in terms of two overall structures of predication, "Quanne hic se" (1)—with the adverbial "on rode" perhaps acting as part of the predicate—and "Wel ou hic" (8). Each structure introduces a major part of the poem, and each sets up the need for a series of noun objects. That is, "When I see" is followed by what is seen—Jesus on the cross, Mary and John, etc. Even though the repeated conjunction *and* tends to link Jesus to the

---

2. Concerning these three lines, see also Manning, *Wisdom*, p. 142.

other things the narrator sees, Jesus acts as the focal point for everything. Mary and John have their existence in terms of him and function, grammatically at least, as do his *rig* and *side*. The coordinate
constructions that create the several direct objects are actually not in
the form of a group of nouns linked by conjunctions. Rather, after
Jesus is mentioned in line 2, the *and*'s introduce a series of verbal
phrases centering around an infinitive (*stonden*) and two past participles (*isuongen, istungen*). The speaker says, "When I see Jesus
on the cross, and (when I see) Mary and John standing beside him,
and (when I see) Jesus' back beaten, and (when I see) his side
pierced (and know that it is all) for the love of man, then . . . ," and
we are ready for the second part of the poem. Along with polysynde-
ton, there is thus in this syntax, with its implied repetition, something
of the rhetorical device of anaphora, which builds up to a climax
(*gradatio*), one that has already been seen in terms of the supra-
segmental features of the passage.

The second part continues using coordinate verbal structures: "I
ought to weep and (I ought to) forsake sin" (8–9). But the word
wel beginning this part is somewhat ambiguous. On the one hand, it
may be a conjunctive adverb, meaning "certainly" or "of course"; on
the other hand, it may function as an adverb of degree—both qualitative and quantitative—referring to how the narrator should *wepen*
and *forleten*. With the repeated three lines at the end an additional
syntactic structure enters the poem. Up to line 10, as has been seen,
the development has been in the form of a relatively simple, though
extended, "when-then" construction in two clauses. But with line 10,
"Yif hic of luue kan," another clause comes in, a dependent one
qualifying the independent clause of lines 8–9, and introducing a
conditional element that tends to shift the focal point of the poem.
This new "Yif hic" clause, reinforcing the overall hypotactic structure
of the lyric, is not directed at the same object that the narrator had
been looking at since the first line. It is not about Jesus or the crucifixion but rather about the narrator, the *hic* himself. There is no
doubting the reality of either the crucifixion or of what the narrator
should do; but there is a doubt about the reality and quality of the
narrator's love. Does he know "real love," here without question
Christ's *luue of man* (7)? Is this love an *imitatio* of Christ's love, an
expression of the Christian concept of *caritas;* or is it an inadequate
amor sui, a love of self that will keep the narrator from being saved?
Furthermore, does the narrator really know (*kan*) love, or does he
exist in the shadow? The shift from the vision of Christ, the thing that
is known, to the narrator, the self that is doubted, serves not to lessen

the vision of the crucifixion but to make meaningful the moral *doctryne* of the poem.

Finally, it should be noted that aspects of medieval number symbolism may well be relevant in this poem. The threefold repetition of the final line may suggest the elevated or pure nature of the love, in that 3 is the number most associated with things of the spirit. Similarly, the total number of lines in the poem may intentionally be 12; for this number was viewed as standing for totality, the combination of this world and the other world, or of man and Christ.[3] Such symbolism would be appropriate here even aside from the mystical nature of the poem, for its author is clearly making use of structural patterns and shaping devices of all sorts to create a concise and yet very connotative piece of literature.

---

3. See, e.g., Hugh of Saint Victor, *De scripturus et scriptoribus sacris*, xv (*PL* 175:22–23).

Worldes blisce, haue god day!
Nou fram min herte wand away;
Him for to louen min hert his went,
4   That thurgh his side spere rent,
His herte blod ssadde for me;
Nayled to the harde tre,
That swete bodi was ytend,
8   Prened wit nayles thre.

Ha, Iesu! Thin holi hefd
Wit ssarpe thornes was byweued;
Thi feyre neb was al bispet
12   Wit spot and blod meynd al bywet;
Fro the crune to the to
Thi body was ful of pine and wo,
And wan and red.

16   Ha, Iesu! Thi smarte ded
Be my sseld and my red
Fram deueles lore.
Ha, suete Iesu, thin hore!
20   For thine pines sore,
Thech min herte right loue the,
Hwas herte blod was ssed for me.

Corpus Christi Coll., Camb. MS 8, p. 457 (on fly leaf, written as prose).
Index, no. 4221, p. 677.

Editions:
Brown, *13*, no. 58, p. 114.

ACCOMPANIED IN MANUSCRIPT by musical notes, this song may be in the form of a carol, with its first two lines acting as a burden; but because of such complications as the irregular stanza arrangement, it is difficult to see just how the refrain would be used. As the poem stands, the first two lines may best be seen as an introduction to stanza 1 and as a basis for the turning to Jesus detailed in stanzas 2 and 3. These two lines, in the form of a direct address, say farewell to *worldes blisce* and demand that the narrator be freed from delight in things of this world. The narrator has now replaced love of the world with love of Jesus, and the rest of the poem acts to justify this change by dwelling on Christ's love of man and on his sacrifice for him. But as this apostrophe presents the situation, it is worldly bliss that must turn away from man, not the other way around. The narrator is here the center of the action, the norm, and he chooses what will affect him.

After this address to *worldes blisce* the narrator states in the next two lines, without explicitly naming Jesus, who it is that now deserves his love: "Him for to louen min hert his went, / That thurgh his side spere rent" (3–4). The response here is to *agape;* it is based on an awareness of the extent of Christ's love for man. And line 5 brings out clearly the narrator's realization of Christ's sacrifice and of man's subsequent responsibility: "His herte blod ssadde for me." This line is clearly a continuation of the thought begun in the previous couplet, and together the three lines illustrate the main principle used in this first stanza to develop the thought. That is, after the initial couplet the stanza develops in terms of three-line units. Lines 3–5 are best viewed as a rhyming tetrameter couplet—structurally the same as the first two lines of the poem—followed by a trimeter line that picks up the rhyme of the initial couplet. The unifying theme of these three lines is the pouring out of Christ's blood through the gash in his side, a symbol of his sacrifice.

The crucifixion itself is referred to only in the next three lines (6–8)—structurally like lines 3–5—where the nailing of Christ to the cross, stated twice, is used to emphasize Christ's agony and thus make us aware not only of the sacrifice but also of the suffering that accompanied it: "Nayled to the harde tre, / That swete bodi was ytend, / Prened wit nayles thre." The fact of the sacrifice is made more meaningful through the focus on such verbs as *nayled* (6), *ytend* (made to suffer, 7), and *prened* (pierced, 8); while such particulars as *harde tre* (6) and *nayles thre* (8) make the suffering vivid and thereby especially significant to us. The metrical form of this last three-line grouping (6–8) is different from that of the preceding one. Although both groupings show a 443 stress pattern, this latter one rhymes *aba* —instead of *aab*—with the *b* rhyme, *ytend*, being a variant of the *went-rent b* rhyme of the stanza itself. The result is not only an intricate rhyme pattern that unifies and develops the stanza but a pattern in which only two rhymes are used to present a rather detailed picture of both the crucifixion and the psychological change taking place within the narrator. Also the initial dramatic effect of the apostrophe to *worldes blisce* is sublimated in the shift of focal point to Christ; and the bulk of the stanza moves from the present, becoming, as it were, a re-creation in narrative form of the crucifixion.

This shift to Christ allows the poet to begin his next two stanzas with a direct address to Jesus, who is now certainly as real as *worldes blisce*—which apparently needed no descriptive comment; and in these stanzas Christ's pain and sacrifice continue to be emphasized. In stanza 2, the first utterance, *Ha, Iesu!*, sets the subject and tone for what follows. *Ha* is most probably to be read as "Ah," a sigh, rather than an exclamation, suggesting the narrator's sense of sympathy and commiseration. As stanza 1 stated how Christ's *swete bodi* (7) suffered, so stanza 2 focuses on Jesus' *holi hefd* (9). And again the verbs of action make vivid the bloody scene. From the head torn by thorns the camera's eye of the narrator closes on the face, *feyre neb*, that was all *bispet* (spat upon, 11); and the resulting intermingling of *spot and blod* (12) is seen to cover the body "Fro the crune to the to," from head to foot. Furthermore, the agony is restated as, and identified with, *pine and wo* (14) and with *wan and red* (15).

The structure of this second stanza is in terms of tetrameter couplets, the two-line movement continuing to the final dimeter line, "And wan and red." Describing the mixture of paleness and blood, this line may be seen not only as concluding the final couplet of the stanza but in actuality as providing the ending for each of the three couplets in the stanza—functioning like the rhetorical devices of zeugma (*adjunctio*)—making them into something like the triads seen in stanza 1. This line thus describes the result of the *ssarpe thornes* that *by-weued*, "wrapped around," the head (10); it also restates the mixture of *spot and blod* (12), shifting from the liquids to their hues; and it finally dramatizes in color the resulting *pine and wo* (14). The method in this stanza thus seems to be to describe Christ's agony in three ways, each of which is culminated in the markedly short final line of the stanza, "And wan and red," a line that gives the impression of saying all that needs to be said.

As stanza 2 focused on the pain, so the final stanza concentrates on the sacrifice, on how these pains allow Christ to act as man's redeemer. The parallelism with stanza 2 is supported by the interjection, *Ha, Iesu!* (16), which likewise begins this stanza, even though the rest of the line, referring to *thi smarte ded,* assumes that the "painful death" or "deed" is known to and understood by the audience. Consequently, lines 16–18 reveal the narrator continuing to address Jesus, who is now the ascendant Christ. His sacrifice is seen as man's—or, more accurately, the narrator's own—shield and counsel (*red,* 17), which can keep him from the doings of the devil. These are, interestingly, described as *deueles lore* (17), "teaching" or "instruction," as opposed, so it would seem, to the actual and tangible act of Christ's sacrifice. The devil can use only *lore* to try to deceive mankind; he has nothing so vivid or meaningful as a concrete action or sacrifice to give his case point and meaning.

Line 19 repeats the address to Christ—"Ha, suete Iesu, thin hore!" —although adding the qualitative *suete.* Now *sseld,* the physical aid, and *red,* the intellectual assistance, come together as *hore,* "grace" or "blessing," the spiritual substance. After the initial three-line unit (16–18), which recalls the method of stanza 1, the poem moves in terms of couplets, as in stanza 2, although possibly line 19 is to be seen as a self-contained unit interjected in the middle of this stanza, standing apart from the thoughts on either side but at the same time leading to the one following it: "For thine pines sore, / Thech min herte right loue the, / Hwas herte blod was ssed for me" (20–22). In substance and actual wording these final three lines return to stanza 1, especially to lines 3–5, where the *pines sore* were first described. Now at the end of the poem the narrator asks Christ to teach (*thech,* 21) his heart true love, that is, to attract and direct his heart now that it is emptied of *worldes blisce.* And, as in stanza 1, though here more noticeably, there is a link between the narrator's *herte* (21) and the *herte blod* of Christ that was shed for him (22). In fact, the last line almost duplicates line 5—"His herte blod ssade for me"—which was the first trimeter, as well as the first finalizing line in the poem. To learn love becomes the narrator's main concern, and his monologue becomes an urgent prayer to Christ to save him, not, as in other poems, because of his fear of hell, but because of his sense of obligation to Christ.

Structurally, the last stanza is different from either of the others. Its initial triad (16–18), with a stress pattern of 442 and a rhyme scheme of *aab,* may be seen as mirrored in a sense in the 334, *bcc* of the final triad (20–22). Between these triads stands line 19, a tetrameter in *b* rhyme. In its use of triads this stanza may be closest to stanza 1, but even in this respect its varied stress pattern distinguishes it.

All three stanzas are, however, related in terms of their development and their rhymes. Such a relationship of rhymes is found in stanza 3, where the initial rhyme /ed/ represents a continuation of the *a* rhyme of stanza 2, also found in the last line of that stanza; the final rhyme of the third stanza, /ey/ then returns to the dominant *a* rhyme of stanza 1.

The most noticeable structural technique of the three stanzas, however, is the use of a single passage to act as a pivotal point for the complete stanza. In stanza 1, the passage is the initial apostrophe to *worldes blisce* (1–2); in stanza 2, it is the final line, "And wan and red" (15), that, as was stated, may be viewed as terminating each of the three couplets in the stanza. And in stanza 3, the structural and pivotal focal point is "Ha, suete Iesu, thin hore!" (19). This exclamation, initially a combination of the *Ha, Iesu's* of lines 9 and 16, also represents in its second part a transformation of the concern about Christ's suffering. Beginning in stanza 2, the narrator addresses himself to various parts of Christ—*thin holi hefd* (9), *thi feyre neb* (11), and *thi body* (14). Now, moving from *thi smarte ded* (16), the narrator exclaims, *thin hore!* (19), as he feels the grace and blessing that come from all the suffering. The following *thin pines sore* (20) represents a summary of the specific hurts detailed in stanza 2, and the term is used to lead to love (21). It is *for* or because of these pains that the narrator feels and understands the need for the love.

It is strange that this rich poem is not better known; it is collected only by Brown and is missing in all recent anthologies and in all criticism of Middle English lyrics. While the subject matter of all explicitly religious lyrics is bound to be stereotyped, a treatment such as this shows how original and effective the total effort can be.

Nou sprinkes the sprai—
Al for loue icche am so seeke
That slepen i ne mai!

4 Als i me rode this endre dai
O mi pleyinge,
Seih i hwar a litel mai
Bigan to singge:
8 "The clot him clingge!
Wai es him i louue-longinge
Sal libben ai!
Nou sprinkes the sprai," &c.

Son icche herde that mirie note,
12 Thider i drogh;
I fonde hire in an herber swot
Under a bogh,
With ioie inogh.
16 Son i asked, "Thou mirie mai,
Hwi sinkes-tou ai
Nou sprinkes the sprai," &c.

Than answerde that maiden swotc,
Midde wordes fewe:
20 "Mi lemman me haues bihot
Of louue trewe;
He chaunges anewe.
Yiif i mai, it shal him rewe
Bi this dai!
Nou sprinkes the sprai," &c.

OF THE GENRE termed the *chanson d'aventure*, this poem is also one of the earliest lyrics recorded unmistakably in the form of a carol, that is, having uniform stanzas and being accompanied by a burden. And, although existing only in a corrupt manuscript, it is also one of the most provocative of the explicitly secular lyrics to come down to us.

Really the report of an encounter between the speaker, the *i* of the poem, and a girl he overhears one day as he is out on his *pleyinge* (5), the poem makes good use of the two points of view, shifting from one to the other and progressing dramatically to its unexpected conclusion. The ending tends to surprise us by jarring with the atmosphere and tone of happiness and fulfillment that had been emphasized throughout the earlier lines. It is only with the last lines that we are aware of how much the narrator's *pleyinge* has colored his and our response to the situation, how, in effect, he and we have erroneously thought of the girl and her song in terms of *pleyinge*. Although we may have been bewildered when we heard the beginning of her song —"The clot him clingge!" (8)—we are soon assured by the narrator that these words represent a *mirie note* (11), and that they are sung by a *mirie mai* (16) who, as she dwells in her *herber swot* (13), has *ioie inogh* (15). Such emphasis on happiness and joy deceives us into forgetting our initial puzzlement at the expression "The clot him clingge!" and the subsequent lines of her song. Our wonder returns only when the grief and anger felt by the girl are detailed unambiguously in the last stanza of the poem.

The narrator here is similar to the naive narrator found in Chaucer's early dream visions. This is the man who does not seem to

---

Lincoln's Inn MS Hale 135, fol. 138v.
Index, no. 360, p. 59; *Supplement*, p. 43.

Editions:
> Brown, *13*, no. 62, pp. 119–20.
> Sisam, p. 163.
> Davies, no. 19, pp. 77–78.
> Stevick, *One*, no. 25, p. 36.
> Greene, *EEC*, no. 450, p. 305; *SEC*, no. 94, pp. 161–62.

Criticism:
> Skeat, W. W., "Fragment of a Middle English Poem," *MLR*, 5 (1910), 104–05.
> Sandison, Helen E., *The "Chanson d'aventure" in Middle English* (Bryn Mawr, Pa., 1913), pp. 47–48.
> Wells, p. 497.
> Wilson, *Early*, p. 263.
> Moore, pp. 58–59.

understand the nature or meaning of what he is experiencing. Like the narrator in the *Book of the Duchess*, for instance, who apparently does not understand the grief of the Man in Black, this narrator provides what turns out to be a wrong interpretation and one that deceives us. In seeing through his eyes and hearing through his ears, we also tend to understand through his interpretations. We expect to be able to believe him, but we find that, rather than be a proper guide, he deludes us by making everything seem innocuous. Through making use of such a false interpreter, the poet is able to change a commonplace, even hackneyed, lament for lost love into a striking and meaningful cry from the heart, one that catches us unaware and makes us respond, perhaps even in spite of ourselves.

As the burden exists at the beginning of the lyric, it seems to express a traditional, even formulaic, kind of love-insomnia. The inconsequential nature of the love-longing is suggested by the light, almost bouncing rhythm of the three lines comprising the refrain as they exist by themselves, separated, that is, from the context of the three stanzas. Even the contrast contained in the burden between blooming nature—"Nou sprinkes the sprai"—and the sad narrator seems artificial and ineffectual until the poem develops and allows the burden to take on additional point. For instance, the garden setting—"I fonde hire in an herber swot" (13)—containing *ioie inogh* (15), suggests the fulfillment of nature. There is a distinct sense of the full, as opposed to the incomplete and the lacking. And the only inadequacy is man who, rather than burst forth with health and vitality—like the *sprai* that *sprinkes* forth (1)—is *seeke* and in a state between sleeping and waking (2–3).

Moreover, the sickness that is mentioned in the burden seems to be only a formula, something that we hardly even consider taking seriously. It seems too much a pose, and, while the narrator himself—if he is also to be viewed as the *i* of the burden—is a *poseur*, the girl definitely is not. While the narrator dallies on his *pleyinge*, she experiences real grief and makes the cliché called love-sickness into something real and serious. The narrator also appears as a fop unable to respond perceptively or with feeling, and his superficial descriptive phrases—for instance, *mirie note, mirie mai*—along with his *pleyinge*, clash with the violent threats and curses uttered by the girl. In her sorrow we see another, though much more real, emptiness that marks human life and that seems very much out of place in so luxuriant a natural setting. Here setting and character lack congruity, and the casual juxtaposition of health and death, joy and sorrow, fulfillment and frustration, laxity and intensity, reveal the paradoxical nature of existence and man's being out of tune with the harmonious world around him.

At the end of the poem there is no return to the narrator. His response could only resemble ours—shock at the extremity of feeling and at the hate that began as love, and perhaps a feeling of embarrassment both at the breakdown of decorum caused by the maiden's words and at the fact that such ugliness and harshness could be present in the midst of life and nature. But this feeling is, of course, the ironic point of the poem; and since we, narrator surrogates, feel it, there is no need to return to him who was at best an inadequate spokesman. At the same time, there is the sense that the harsh reality which comes out in the girl's forthright expression causes the puffed-up narrator to explode and disappear.

While the poem tends to move away from the carefree and light to the harsh and grating, it also makes us aware of the difference between appearance and reality. We never quite know where we are throughout most of the poem, or how we should view certain phrases like the expression of the girl's feelings in lines 8–10. This song is what is explained later in the poem, although it is only after the third stanza that we really understand it. The line, "The clot him clingge!" (8), sounds at first like a statement of fact, not like a subjunctive or imperative—indeed, the manuscript reads *clingges*, which, as the rhyme word, seems to be erroneous. What is more, the meanings of individual words in the line are not clear. Both *clot* and *clingge* are ambiguous, even when we understand the construction as meaning "May the clot cling to him," for we may think that the maiden is saying that her lover is dead or that, now that he is dead, let him be buried. The difficulty may be seen in the way one editor glosses the line "May the earth (of the grave) stick to him (?), waste him."[1]

Similarly, the next two lines of the song are syntactically confusing: "Wai es him i louue-longinge / Sal libben ai" (9–10). One interpretation of them may be that they are in the form of a curse at or imprecation against the lover who has caused the girl to sorrow. But the form *wai es* does not readily support the imperative or subjunctive mood that would necessarily exist in a "Woe be to" construction. Furthermore, it would appear that the *him* of line 9 is not the same as the *him* of 8, and that the lines are not talking about a desire that the unfaithful lover should experience love-longing. Rather, the *him* in 9 most likely means the more general term "person," and may be seen acting in opposition to the lover referred to in

---

1. Davies, p. 77.

line 8. Lines 9–10 may best be translated as referring to the maiden herself and to the rejection of her love: "Unhappy is the person (*wai es him*) who must live always in love-longing." In this sense the previous line, "The clot him clingge," could even be taken as the expected outcome of such unhappiness—death, as it were, from a broken heart.

At this point in the poem the only thing clear is that the words are ambiguous. The ambiguity continues and is even reinforced in the next stanza as the narrator's emphasis on the merry and sweet—an expression we only later realize to be artificial and foolish—contrasts paradoxically with the atmosphere of *wai* that has been created by the girl's sorrow. But neither the narrator nor we are prepared for the girl's subsequent vehemence, as revealed in the third stanza. After lines 20–22 explain the reasons for her anger—"Mi lemman me haues bihot / Of louue trewe; / He chaunges anewe"—the last two lines of the poems explicitly express her attitude toward his infidelity: "Yiif i mai, it shal him rewe / Bi this dai!" (23–24). Taking "Bi this dai" not as an affirmative but as a meaningful part of the utterance begun in the previous line,[2] we may read the passage as "If I can (contrive it), this day will make him repent of what he has done." The passive-seeming, helpless little *mirie mai* becomes something entirely different to us, although we now realize that she has been this way all along, and that we have failed to understand her, her emotions, and even the situation.

The poem constantly presents us with the unexpected, not the least of which is the girl herself who, from the beginning, does not act as the narrator expects. And even when we understand her sorrow and realize that her "herber swot / Under a bogh" (13–14) may be a symbolic grave, we are still not prepared for her attitudes. She is out of place in the environment of the poem and may even represent something supernatural in the midst of nature—a witch, as it were, preparing a spell. Still, once we accept her grief and anger, we might well expect her to talk of dying—there is certainly something unhealthy about her brooding and cursing; but, strangely, she talks of living (*libben*, 10), moreover, of living forever (*ai*). This sense of permanence contrasts ironically with the later line about her false lover: "He chaunges anewe" (22).

The poem develops in terms of three generally parallel stanzas of seven lines plus burden. The usual metrical pattern is a quatrain composed of alternating four-stressed and two-stressed lines, overflowing, as it were, into another two-stressed line. The rhyme pattern of these

---

2. See Skeat, p. 105.

five lines is *ababb*. The sixth and seventh lines of each stanza, in *bc* rhyme, except for lines 16–17, return to the alternating four-stress, two-stress pattern. This then trails off in the burden—joined to the stanza through continuing the *c* rhyme—with its lines of two, three (or possibly four), and three stresses. The stanzas are further joined together by a complexity of subordinate clauses and by certain key subordinating conjunctions and adverbs. For instance, *als* in the initial line of the first stanza (4) leads in one sense to *son* (as soon as) in the first line of the second stanza (12)—a word which is repeated in line 16, although there it means "at once"—and the whole movement culminates with *than* in the first line of stanza 3 (18). But periodically punctuating this pattern is *nou*, from the first line of the burden, giving a sense of immediacy that contrasts with the reporting of past actions seen in the three stanzas.

There are actually four distinct actions taking place, being reported, or being projected in this poem. First is the reported experience of the narrator, told in the past tense; second is the actual situation of the girl's singing, including the dialogue created by the narrator; third is the past action of the lover's infidelity, described in the present-perfect tense; and fourth is the projected trouble, even death, for the false love, described generally in present subjunctive and future indicative. But all these actions, even those in past and future, go on in the foreground of the piece. In the background is blossoming nature—"Nou sprinkes the sprai"—an actual movement of life that is ironically opposed to the immediate stultifying sorrow and to the projected death.

Although there exists a parallel French text that contains a fourth stanza recording the poet's successful wooing of the girl,[3] this text is not the immediate source of the Middle English poem, and we should not necessarily conclude that the English poem must also have had another stanza that is now lost. Such a stanza is not only unnecessary to the sense or completeness of the lyric, but with its happy ending it would tend to destroy the suggestiveness and irony that are the work's most compelling qualities.

---

3. Sandison, pp. 47–48n.

Erthe toc of erthe, erthe wyth woh,
Erthe other erthe to the erthe droh,
Erthe leyde erthe in erthene throh—
Tho heuede erthe of erthe erthe ynoh.

Harley MS 2253, fol. 59v. (cf. Harl. 913, fol. 62).
Index, no. 3939, p. 631; *Supplement,* p. 451.

Editions:
   Murray, Hilda M., ed., *Erthe upon Erthe,* EETS OS 141 (London, 1911),
      pp. xvff., esp. p. 1.
   Brown, *13,* no. 73, p. 132.
   Stevick, *One,* no. 26, p. 37.
   Brook, no. 1, p. 29.

Criticism:
   Kane, pp. 122–23.
   Woolf, pp. 84–85.

BASED ON THE WELL-KNOWN "dust to dust" idea as found in Genesis
3:19—*"pulvis es, et in pulverem reverteris"*—and in Ecclesiastes 3:20,
as well as in the liturgy for Ash Wednesday, this poem presents a
theme very popular in medieval verse. Resembling that motif which
appears in such forms as the Dance of Death and the Debate between
the Body and the Soul, this treatment, called the Earth upon Earth
theme, seems to be originally English. It exists only in Middle English
texts, except for one parallel Latin translation; and the particular
poem quoted here probably represents the earliest text of one of the
two extant versions.[1]

The lyric also resembles, and may actually be thought of as, a
typical Middle English verse riddle. In this *aenigmata*, as in others
of the kind, the first problem is to understand just what the words are
saying. It seems that here *erthe* is being used in two ways or that the
single term *erthe* is made to stand for two different entities. By using
the same term to refer to two things, the poet has created an ambiguity
and has given his poem a dominant paradoxical complexity. If we see
that one *erthe* refers to that which is created from the other, the
difficulty decreases. One *erthe*, say *erthe^a*, may consequently be read
as meaning the microcosm "man," and the other—call it *erthe^b*—is to
be understood as the macrocosm "Mother Earth," or an equivalent of
the larger element from which man is formed. There still remains the
problem of seeing which *erthe* is being referred to each of the twelve
times the term—or, in one instance, *erthene* (3), a variation of it—is
used. And before we can attempt a paraphrase of the four lines comprising the poem, we must make certain that we understand the meanings of all the other terms.

This second problem mainly concerns the verbs, most immediately
toc (1). It may seem to be a simple preterite meaning "took," but
such a straight-forward rendering does not really work. Should we
say that the first phrase—"Erthe toc of erthe"—means that *erthe^b*
(that is, earth itself) took from *erthe^b* (again earth itself), we are
faced with the difficulty of having earth acting in and of itself as a
creator of sorts. If, on the other hand, we take the phrase to mean
that *erthe^a* (man) took from *erthe^b* (earth), we have the opposite
but similar problem whereby man must be viewed as a creator. The
other two possibilities here—earth took from man, and man took from
man—are meaningless. The problem is easily solved, however, if we
view *toc* not as a simple preterite but as a past participle—even though
participial forms of *take* seem always to have been distinct from pret-

---

1. Murray, p. ix.

erite forms. The phrase would then read, "Man taken from earth," paralleling what appears in another Middle English lyric on this theme, "Erthe oute of erthe."[2] Keeping the particular *erthes* in mind, we may then restate the first line as "Man taken from earth, man with wrong," with the last phrase perhaps suggesting man's sinful nature, though there is some difficulty here. *Woh*, besides meaning "harm" or "wrong" (OE *woh*), may also signify "woe" (OE *wá*) and refer to both the suffering of birth and the hardship of man's life in the post-lapsarian world he inhabits.

The next line—"Erthe other erthe to the erthe droh"—may then be read as "Earth drew the other earth (that is, man) to itself, ostensibly referring to man's death and burial. What follows is more ambiguous: "Erthe leyde erthe in erthene throh." Whereas the second *erthe* seems clearly to refer to man, the first *erthe* may mean either "men"—*erthe*[a] as a collective noun—or "earth"; either reading makes sense. This *erthe* laid man in an earthen coffin, the burial representing the apparent drawing to death seen in line 2, as well as its result. At the same time, the relationship between lines 2 and 3 may be more in the form of a cause and effect. Together the lines may suggest that man, who is drawn to things of this world (2), will ultimately be imprisoned in this world, even to the extent of being indentified with earth. Suggested may be the futility of man's "drawing to" the earth instead of reaching toward heaven, of his striving to amass wealth, which will ironically be what finally kills him.

The final line is still more complicated: "Tho heuede erthe of erthe erthe ynoh." It could mean "Then man had enough earth from earth," this last being the earth in which he is interred; or "Then earth had enough earth from man"—that is, the body composed of earth which was brought to and put in the earth. In any case, *ynoh* functions to suggest a surfeit—as though man's greed or gluttony is viewed as the sin of earth, which acts even to choke man—and the acts of death and burial are seen only as inadequate. That which has come from the earth returns to it, but the return is neither welcome nor productive. The point of this last line may be clearly understood by looking at the last stanza of "Erthe oute of erthe," the poem on the same theme already mentioned:

> Now why that erthe luffes erthe, wondere me thinke,
> Or why that erthe for erthe scholde other swete or swinke;

---

2. Chambers and Sidgwick, no. 94, p. 171; Davies, no. 87, p. 180. See also the several other examples in Murray.

For when that erthe appon erthe is broghte within brinke,
Than shall erthe of erthe hafe a foulle stinke.[3]

At the same time, the poem asks us to question the nature or, more exactly, the worth of man himself who comes from the earth only—perhaps because of his desire for riches—to return finally to it and become again part of it. The confusion of the various *erthes* seems designed not merely to complicate matters but to suggest that after all there may be no essential difference between the physical man who inclines after the world and the physical world that attracts him. And this world (*erthe*[b]) is not revealed as any kind of dynamic principle or living force; it is no *Natura naturans*. Even though earth apparently became man, the poem is hardly concerned with the coming of life. Rather, it focuses on the return of man to earth, with the transference of form being seen as something resembling death.

In medieval literature, especially in those writings on august subjects, as Woolf rightly points out, verbal ambiguities were thought of as "a rhetorical means of revealing underlying correspondences," as "linguistic indications of the intricate unity of the divine plan."[4] In this poem, though human life and death may not seem especially august, the wit seems designed to create paradox and ambiguity. Moreover, the harsh sounds, heavy stresses, and irregular meter that mark these four lines all work to emphasize the inherent unpleasantness of the subject. The lines may best be described as four-stressed and, in the manner of traditional alliterative verse, may be seen as subdivided into half-lines of two stresses each, with a caesura between. Such a description appears to be more in harmony with the sense of the poem than the reading that views the lines as pentameters, even though it is clear that the first half-lines—all ending, it would seem, after the second *erthe*, and all thus rhyming exactly—have more syllables than the second, as well as an additional partial stress. In line 1, the half-line is clearly distinguished because of the appositive kind of construction; in lines 2 and 3 the caesura is not so pronounced; and in the final line it is hardly apparent at all, perhaps being determined by the impression given in the other lines.[5] Probably the best way of viewing this poem is as a combination of alliterative and metrical techniques.

The first three stresses of each line is on *erthe*—or *erthene*—and

---

3. Chambers and Sidgwick, ibid.; see also Davies, ibid., and Murray, passim.
4. Woolf, p. 85.
5. The poem may be seen with these caesurae in Murray, e.g., p. xv.

the final stress is on the last syllable of the line, the harsh *-oh*, phonetically an open *o*, followed by a glottal fricative [ɔx]. The second
and fourth stresses would seem to be slightly heavier than the first
and third, and, with the first half-line containing more syllables than
the second, there develops a slowing down, a sense of heaviness, even
of finality, as the lines go from the feminine endings before the caesura to the masculine end rhymes. The tendency to heaviness is reinforced by the several other syllables that demand at least partial
stress.

Line 1, for instance—"Erthe toc of erthe, erthe wyth woh"—might
appear to be composed of five trochaic and iambic feet, but it should
probably be read as containing four primary stresses, with *toc* receiving a secondary or tertiary stress. Also, if the final *-e*'s of *erthe* are
to be pronounced—except where, as in *erthe other* (2), they precede a
vowel—the line may be seen metrically as containing in its first half-
line an amphimace of sorts and an amphibrach; then in the second
half-line a trochee is followed by an iamb: /X\|X/X||/X|X/. There
is no dominant metrical pattern here, nor is there in the other three
lines of the poem. As I view the patterns of the next two lines, they
look like this: line 2—/\|X/X||XX/|X/—and line 3—/X/||X||X/|XX/.

The harshness begun in line 1 continues unabated in these two
central lines and reaches a high point in line 4, which is both the most
ambiguous line of the poem and the most metrically awkward: "Tho
heuede erthe of erthe erthe ynoh." Breaking the anaphoric pattern
created in the earlier three lines through their opening with *erthe*,
this fourth line begins a conclusion. But this conclusion takes the
form of a noticeable breakdown of rhythm. In particular, the division into half-lines is not clear, and there is a problem of syncope in
heuede. If, as suggested above, the caesura comes after the second
erthe, the first half-line, with its partial stresses, seems excessively
long and involved. But with *heuede* taken as monosyllable, the line
may be scanned as follows: \X/|X/X||/X|/. Produced is an unpleas-
ant cacophony, and when we reach the final *erthe ynoh*, with its incomplete final foot, we sense what is meant by *erthe* as a destructive
thing. Just as we have had enough of the intentional heaviness and
awkwardness of sound and rhythm, so we have had enough of *erthe*.

The fact that this poem is in four lines with four dominant stresses
in each line may be significant since in medieval numerology the
number four was the traditional number for earth, things physical and
man,[6] just as three was the number of the spirit. But while the earthly

---

6. See, e.g., Augustine, *In Johannis Evangelium*, ix. 14 (*PL* 35:1465), and
Vincent F. Hopper, *Medieval Number Symbolism* (New York, 1938), esp. p. 84.

and spiritual are often joined together—as four and three produce the especially significant numbers seven and twelve—here four remains alone. The emphasis is entirely on things of earth, on man as a creature produced from it, who can look forward only to returning to it—at least if he continues to be a creature immersed in it. Man is not seen here in God's image, and there is no explicit future for him other than the earth. In fact, life tends to be negated, and though there is a cycle presented here, it is one with death as its end, perhaps with death also as its beginning—the initial act of line 1 is done *wyth woh*. Everything is unrelieved and unpleasant, and we are glad when this piece ends.

We should, however, still recognize the artistry that has gone into the lyric, an artistry in some ways similar to that found in a later Middle English cycle-poem that is also something of a riddle:

> Pees maketh plente,
> Plente maketh pryde,
> Pryde maketh plee,
> Plee maketh pouert,
> Pouert makethe pees.[7]

Over before we realize it, the piece takes us unaware, and we may be surprised to find that we have ended back where we started. We do not realize what the poem is doing, even though everything in the five lines seems to be working to make us see the relationship between the substantives—they all use /p/ alliteration; the verb is the same in each line, not distracting us; and the same word ending one line begins the next, except for *pees*, though, of course, the last line leads to the first and to another reading of the lines. There is a continual circle here, a vicious one in the sense that it shows that nothing can really be accomplished. The good and the bad are intertwined, one leading unexpectedly to the other: peace leads to plenty, which leads in turn to pride of possessions, which causes strife, which results again in peace. Although the poem withholds an explicit judgment of this cycle, we sense that it is being very ironic, especially so because everything seems so innocuous and even pleasant.

While this lyric makes its point by deceiving us with its smoothness, "Erthe toc of erthe" is brutally harsh and, for all its ambiguities, quite frank in its message. No one listening to it—even if he did not know Middle English—could fail to sense the disgust, contempt, and bitterness inherent in it. Perhaps ultimately to be seen in the *con-*

---

7. Camb. Univ. MS Ff.I.6, fol. 53v. See Robbins, *Sec*, no. 84, p. 81.

temptus mundi tradition, it nevertheless fails to move to anything above or beyond the dirt and the grave. The oblique statement and understatement revealed in the last line do not amuse us but seem like the smile of someone watching a hanging. And, indeed, in his indirectness and intellectual ambiguity the poet is detached from his subject and from us. What he has produced has thus the effect of both sermon and riddle. He is telling his audience something, implicitly showing them the need to look to heaven; but he is also amusing himself, as it were, by disguising what he is saying—as was the case in "Pees maketh plente"—so that one must work to find out the point. While this is a bothersome poem, it is certainly a compelling one.

Bytuene Mersh and Aueril
Whan spray biginneth to springe,
The lutel foul hath hire wyl
4   On hyre lud to synge.
Ich libbe in loue-longinge
For semlokest of alle thynge—
He may me blisse bringe;
8   Icham in hire baundoun.
     An hendy hap ichabbe yhent!
     Ichot from heuene it is me sent—
     From alle wymmen mi loue is lent
12   And lyht on Alysoun.

On heu hire her is fayr ynoh,
Hire browe broune, hire eye blake;
With lossum chere he on me loh,
16   With middel smal and wel ymake.
Bote he me wolle to hire take
For to buen hire owen make,
Longe to lyuen ichulle forsake
20   And feye fallen adoun.
     An hendy hap &c.

Nihtes when y wende and wake—
Forthi myn wonges waxeth won—
Leuedi, al for thine sake,
24   Longinge is ylent me on.
In world nis non so wyter mon
That al hire bounte telle con:
Hire swyre is whittore then the swon,
28   And feyrest may in toune.
     An hendi &c.

Icham for wowyng al forwake,
Wery so water in wore;
Lest eny reue me my make,
32   Ychabbe y-yyrned yore.
Betere is tholien whyle sore
Then mournen euermore.
Geynest vnder gore,
36   Herkne to my roun:
     An hendi &c.

DESCRIBED AS "a poem of delightful freshness and melody" and as "one of the most charming of Middle English songs,"[1] this piece uses a sprightly refrain that sings itself and that is integrally attached to the four stanzas. Even though the poem cannot be considered a carol —there is no indication that it begins with the burden—it is still a call to merriment, even to the dance. The title that modern editors have given it, "Alisoun," may be something of a misnomer; for the main concern is with expressing the narrator's feelings, not with describing a girl. Alisoun is, to be sure, the focal point of these feelings, that which gives them meaning; but the feelings themselves receive the major emphasis throughout the four stanzas and the refrain.

The beginning of the poem is somewhat deceptive. The first quatrain, stating how in springtime birds desire to sing, is an introduction providing a setting and context for what follows: our impression on first reading is to expect the next lines to be the birds' song. But with line 5, we find that it is the narrator who is stating his love-longing. Our reaction to this apparent non sequitur might justifiably be that the poet has provided a contrast between the happiness of the birds in their gay spring setting and the unhappiness of the narrator, who looks for but still lacks *blisse* (7). But then, as the burden closes this stanza, we find unexpectedly that the narrator considers his state to be fortunate. He has received *an handy hap* (a fair fortune, 9) that he knows has come from heaven. Thus, far from ending on a note of despair, the stanza through its sprightly burden is finally an affirma-

---

MS Harley 2253, fol. 63v.
Index, no. 515, p. 83; *Supplement,* p. 58.

Editions:
> Brown, *13,* no. 77, pp. 138–39.
> Chambers and Sidgwick, no. 4, pp. 6–7.
> Brook, no. 4, p. 33.
> Sisam, pp. 165–66.
> Davies, no. 13, pp. 67–68.
> Stevick, *One,* no. 27, pp. 38–40.

Criticism:
> Wells, p. 493.
> Moore, pp. 68–69.
> Speirs, pp. 56–58.
> Dronke, Peter, *Medieval Latin and the Rise of European Love-Lyric,* 2d
>   ed. (Oxford, 1968), 1:121–22.
> Oliver, pp. 22–23.

---

1. Davies, p. 313; Wells, p. 493.

tion of hope and happiness. Faster moving than the lines preceding it, more regularly stressed and in masculine rhyme, this burden introduces a style and tone not hitherto found in the poem.

The impression is that the narrator refuses finally to be troubled by his frustrated love, and the juxtaposition of unhappiness and happiness provides what may even be regarded as a humorous touch. Because of this juxtaposition—and the fact that the concluding note is on happiness and success—we can hardly take the narrator's plight seriously. The juxtaposition continues through the three subsequent stanzas, with the unhappiness becoming increasingly detailed and appearing more and more extreme. But as this unhappiness continues to be followed by the same affirmative refrain, the result is something approaching farce. Neither is the narrator acting in the manner of someone who is suffering, nor is the gay refrain in accord with his hapless complaint.

The second stanza gives the reason for his love-longing. In its first quatrain it presents a detailed portrait of Alisoun: her shapely waist, her fair coloring, her dark eyebrows and black eyes—traditional signs of lechery, also marking the heroine of Chaucer's *Miller's Tale*, likewise named Alisoun.[2] The second group of four lines repeats the narrator's love-longing and stresses how he will die if he cannot have his love. The burden that follows is clearly out of place, but again the lack of humor is apparently for comic purposes. If we take the narrator's lament seriously, it appears at the end of line 20 as though he is on the brink of falling down lifeless (*feye fallen adoun*). To have him then burst into happy-go-lucky song and state his good fortune is clearly an unexpected conclusion and a wrenching of the tone and feeling that have been developing throughout the stanza.

When this song is over, it is as though the music slows down once again, this time to a funereal pace, as the narrator begins the third stanza by detailing his woes, which ironically parallel in reverse the beauties of Alisoun that were listed in the first quatrain of the previous stanza: her *browe broune* (14) and *lossum chere* (15) contrast with his pale cheeks (*wonges*, 22). Whereas alliteration has noticeably marked the previous stanzas—/sp/ (2); /b/ (7, 14); /f/ (20); and especially /l/ (5, 11, 15, 19), which is appropriately the dominant sound in this lilting poem—still, none of the sounds so affects the movement of the poem as the profusion of /w/'s in lines 21–22— "Nihtes when y wende and wake— / Forthi myn wonges waxeth won."

---

2. *Canterbury Tales*, 1 (A), 3245; see George B. Pace, "Physiognomy and Chaucer's Summoner and Alisoun," *Traditio*, 18 (1962), esp. 418–20.

These, echoed by the /w/'s in lines 25 and 27, and reinforced by the many nasals in this third stanza, noticeably slow down the movement and create a sound that is clearly mournful.

The reversal of the second stanza continues in the next four lines (25–28) as the narrator returns to Alisoun's beauties. The word he uses to describe her general qualities, *bounte* (26), is somewhat ambiguous. Generally meaning "goodness" or even "fullness," it would here seem to be used with particular reference to her physical attributes; and indeed in the next line (27) the narrator acts as though he can scarcely refrain from commenting on these. Furthermore, his descriptions become increasingly flowery. In the second stanza he generally used simple adjectives to describe Alisoun's hair, face, and waist. But now, as he focuses—almost in spite of himself—on her neck, he uses a sensuous simile, the first one in the poem: "Hire swyre is whittore then the swon." This is followed by a generalization of how she is *feyrest* of all. Such is the final expression of Alisoun's *bounte*. It shows what about the lady really interests the narrator—in spite of the fact that he refers to *heuene* in his repeated statement of his good fortune.

The last stanza is the slowest moving and saddest of all, and again the /w/'s predominate: "Icham for wowyng al forwake, / Wery so water in wore" (29–30). The movement of the revelation of the narrator's grief has been from a general statement of his *loue-longinge* (5) to his intention to die because of his unrequited love—"Longe to lyuen ichulle forsake / And feye fallen adoun" (19–20)—to his particular acts of tossing and turning at night, which cause—even more particularly—his cheeks to grow pale (22). Now in the fourth stanza the emphasis is on the quality, rather than the fact or the details, of his sorrow. This shift is accomplished by the use of a simile to describe the narrator's lying awake worn out (29–30): he feels as "wery so water in wore," weary as water in a troubled pool or on a beach. That is, he is like the waves helplessly tossed by the wind or tumbling on a shore. Nature here is quite different from what it was in the first stanza when the only motion was that of the slender shoots or twigs beginning to grow or coming into leaf—"spray beginneth to springe" (2). But at this point in the fourth stanza there is clearly no fruition of the love, and the narrator seems pathetically—though humorously —out of tune with the melody of life that is around him and that is celebrated by him in the burden.

His focus on Alisoun and her physical attractions is now replaced by a concern that someone else will get her, implying that he deserves her because he has desired her for a long time—"Ychabbe y-yyerned yore" (32). But even this jealousy gives way to another feeling, contained in the ambiguous assertion that follows: "Betere is tholien whyle sore / Then mournen euermore" (33–34). This is certainly different from the narrator's initial feeling that Alisoun "may me blisse bringe" (7). The implication at the beginning of the poem was that, because she is "semlokest of alle thynge" (6), Alisoun will not allow him to suffer. But in the fourth stanza, with the assertion that "it is better to suffer sorely for a while than to sorrow evermore," there seems to be, in one sense, a loss of hope. That is, we do not really know whether the narrator means that it is better to suffer as he does than to renounce Alisoun and then grieve forever over his giving up something he might possibly have obtained had he persevered. It is equally possible, taking *tholien* and *mournen* as equal and parallel, that the narrator means that he should give up Alisoun since she will bring him only permanent unhappiness. The ambiguity in lines 33–34 is hardly resolved, but it contrasts sharply with the statement of good fortune in the refrain, which at the end of the fourth stanza seems most like empty words.

Still, as the last lines before the final statement of the refrain indicate, the poem changes from being a report about the narrator's feelings to a direct plea to Alisoun: "Geynest vnder gore, / Herkne to my roun" (35–36). Earlier, in line 23, the narrator had addressed Alisoun; but there his words represented only a temporary change of pace, since later in that same stanza he returned to third-person pronouns. At the end of stanza 4 he requests that Alisoun listen to his *roun*, literally "whisper" but figuratively "speech" or even "song." The word *roun* is interesting in that it may make the opening lines of the poem relevant to what has followed. There with the statement of the "lutel foul" desiring to sing (3–4), it appeared as though the song of the bird was going to follow. In other Middle English poems—the lyrics "Lenten ys come with loue to toune" and "The Thrush and the Nightingale," for instance—the bird's song is explicitly called *briddes roune*. Perhaps the narrator here is expressing himself in terms of a bird, or perhaps the whole poem should be viewed as, ironically, the courtly-love sickness of a bird, as something comparable to what is found in Chaucer's *Squire's Tale* or, more humorously, in his *Nun's Priest's Tale*.

In another sense, if the words that follow are really those of the narrator, the poem may be seen as a counterpart to the song of "the lutel foul" (3). Hardly a joyous song, however, it becomes decreasingly celebratory and increasingly dreary; and in the last stanza the narrator's words are presented as something of a final gasp. The exaggeration necessitated by this reading would be, of course, another ludicrous touch, as is the way the narrator addresses Alisoun in his final petition to her—"Geynest vnder gore" (35), literally "fairest under gown." While this phrase is rightly taken by editors and translators to mean "fairest (or kindest) among women" or "fairest of any alive,"[3] the sexual suggestiveness is clear. Throughout the poem the narrator has been thinking of Alisoun in physical terms, and here, in his final words, he cannot refrain from thinking about what is under her *gore*.

The stanzaic patterning of the poem is more intricate than one might at first realize, and reflects the complex sound patterns, as well as the greater complexity of emotions being detailed. Each stanza is divided into three four-line sections, each end-stopped, the last being the burden, which is in all cases joined to the stanzas by the *-oun* rhyme of the line preceding. Whereas the initial quatrain of each stanza has the customary *abab* rhyme scheme, the metrical patterns vary. The quatrains in stanzas 1 and 4 use alternating four-stressed and three-stressed lines, producing something close to typical ballad meter. In stanzas 2 and 3, on the other hand, all the lines of the initial quatrain are four-stressed. These two stanzas consistently use tetrameter; only the line preceding the burden and the final line of the burden are three-stressed. Stanzas 1 and 4, however, reveal many three-stressed lines; indeed, the second quatrain of each stanza contains only one tetrameter line. But this four-stressed line is not in the same place in each: in the first stanza, of lines 5–8, the four-stressed one is the second, line 6; but in the fourth stanza, of lines 33–36, the tetrameter line is the first, line 33.

Such a variation in patterning is not found elsewhere in the meter or rhyme of this poem and may represent an error of scribal transcription. In a patterned quatrain the variable line would most likely come either at the end—as it does in the refrain here, where the last line is in trimeter—or at the beginning, but hardly as the second line. Moreover, the patterning as seen in the initial quatrain of these two stanzas shows the four-stressed line preceding the three-stressed one. Taking this as a model of sorts, we might well conclude that lines 5 and 6 should be reversed, thus producing tetrameter followed by trimeter: "For semlokest of alle thynge, / Ich libbe in louelonginge." The lexical meaning of the two lines would not be af-

---

3. See, e.g., Davies, p. 68, and Stevick, p. 40.

fected; but, more significantly, the ordering of the structure of modification would now be in accord with the customary syntactic pattern of the poem, where the phrase or subordinate clause precedes the independent clause. For instance, likewise in stanza 1, the first quatrain (1–4) begins in its first two lines with a dependent structure. Similarly, the same inverted construction is found in the second quatrain of stanza 2 (17–20), in the first quatrain of stanza 3 (21–22), and in the last two lines of the refrain (11–12).

The first and fourth stanzas are also linked by means of the narrator's feelings, which are expressed throughout the poem in terms of his being acted upon by Alisoun. She is the subject, he the object; he hopes that Alisoun "may *me* blisse bringe" (7); she "on *me* loh" (smiles, 15); he wishes that she will take him to be her true love ("*me* wolle to hire take," 17); longing for Alisoun "is ylent *me* on" (24); and in the refrain, good fortune "is *me* sent" from heaven (10). He is primarily a passive creature helplessly at the mercy of his love. But in stanzas 1 and 4, along with the refrain, he appears, more so than anywhere else in the poem, to assert himself—as the verbs associated with the "I" show: in stanza 1, *ich libbe* (5) and *icham* (8); in stanza 4, *icham* (29) and *ichabbe* (32); and in the refrain *ichabbe* (9) and *ichot* (10). Paradoxically, however, except for the actions of the refrain, these are all assertions of his love-longing and helplessness: for instance, *ich libbe* (5) is followed by *in loue-longinge*, and *icham* (8) by *in hire baundoun*. These represent, nevertheless, the totality of the narrator's actions.

There are only two other comparable assertions in the rest of the poem, but these are essentially different from the constructions in the first and fourth stanzas. The expression *ichulle* (19) is ironically a withdrawal, for the narrator is saying in the context of this assertion that he will forsake life and fall down lifeless unless he receives Alisoun's favors. Also this *ichulle* is part of a subjunctive construction in the future tense, whereas all the other verbs are clearly in the indicative mood and, even when auxiliaries, in the present tense. The second exception is found in the third stanza—*y wende and wake* (21)—but this is likewise different from the assertions of self found in the first and fourth stanzas because here the action of the narrator is reported in a subordinated "when" clause, one that is preliminary to the main clause. But all of these assertions, with the exception of those in the burden, have in common the sense that they are expressions of the narrator's helplessness; and they belie the hope and faith expressed in the burden.

It is pertinent to say a few more words about this burden itself:

> An hendy hap ichabbe yhent!
> Ichot from heuene it is me sent—
> From alle wymmen mi loue is lent
> And lyht on Alysoun.

Although explicitly an assertion of the narrator's good fortune in that his desire has shifted from *alle wymmen* to one woman, Alisoun, the statement may represent a wish-fulfillment rather than an actual fact. The focusing on a single object seen here is apparently different from the life of promiscuity the narrator seems to have led; and although he is jubilant about this shift, he is unbelievably jubilant, especially since, as the developing poem reveals, he has had no success with Alisoun. His fortune must ironically have come from heaven, for it is both making a monogamous lover out of him and giving him a kind of purgatory on earth. In this light the entire statement of the burden may be ironic, or at least may be ironic by the time of its fourth utterance.

This burden also contains the greatest amount of motion in the poem, much more than that of growing plants (2) or that of the tossing and turning lover (21). The narrator has received (*yhent*) a good fortune which has been *sent* to him from heaven: his love is taken away (*lent*) from other women and settled (*lyht*) on Alisoun. The movement of the burden, along with the particular word *lyht*, would be especially appropriate were the refrain to be seen in terms of the hopping of birds, alighting here and there. The "going from-coming to" movement is twice stated, first in terms of the fortune—in a sense, the message—which has come from heaven, then in terms of his love —the response, as it were, to the message. But with his response the movement apparently stops: far from participating in such rhythm, Alisoun cuts it off. She apparently neither receives the love nor responds in any way. And it is this negative response that creates the tossing and turning and the destructive melancholy that is the melody more of death than of life.[4]

---

4. Speaking particularly of this refrain, Dronke writes, "despite language that is almost comic in its homely, quacking sounds, we are confronted with one of the profoundest enigmas of *amour courtois*. To affirm in the same breath 'my destiny is in her hands' and 'I have taken hold of my destiny myself' and 'it has come to me from heaven' (that is from God)—is this not self-contradictory?" Such may be stated, he concludes, because of "a pattern of ideas whereby such a threefold statement is made possible." (*Medieval Latin*, p. 122).

Lenten ys come with loue to toune,
With blosmen and with briddes roune,
   That al this blisse bryngeth.
4 Dayeseyes in this dales,
Notes suete of nyhtegales,
   Vch foul song singeth.
The threstelcoc him threteth oo—
8 Away is huere wynter woo
   When woderoue springeth.
This foules singeth ferly fele,
Ant wlyteth on huere wynne wele,
12   That al the wode ryngeth.

The rose rayleth hire rode,
The leues on the lyhte wode
   Waxen al with wille.
16 The mone mandeth hire bleo,
The lilie is lossom to sco,
   The fenyl and the fille.
Wowes this wilde drakes,
20 Miles murgeth huere makes,
   As strem that striketh stille.
Mody meneth, so doh mo;
Ichot ycham on of tho,
24   For loue that likes ille.

The mone mandeth hire lyht,
So doth the semly sonne bryht,
   When briddes singeth breme;
28 Deawes donketh the dounes,
Deores with huere derne rounes,
   Domes forte deme.
Wormes woweth vnder cloude,
32 Wymmen waxeth wounder proude,
   So wel hit wol hem seme.
Yef me shal wonte wille of on,
This wunne weole y wole forgon,
36   Ant whyt in wode be fleme.

A LOVE SONG in the form of a *reverdie* or salute to the spring, this poem is deceptively simple. It is far more than a detailing of how spring and love affect nature, more than the rhetorical device of amplification known as prolepsis, and more than a collection of stereotyped images and phrases, even though the first six lines are essentially the same as those of another thirteenth-century lyric, "The Thrush and the Nightingale."[1] Its complexity may best be seen in its blending of the language of sound and symbol, in its using restatement—an incremental repetition of sorts—as the means of building to a conclusion, and in its relating the activity of nature to the feelings of man in general and of the narrator in particular. The lyric is structured primarily in terms of triads, each three-line unit containing a couplet in tetrameters followed by a trimeter line that rhymes with the other three trimeter lines in each stanza. Thus the *aabccbddbeeb* pattern of each stanza is able to push along the thought and at the same time, through the *b* rhyme, to link each three-part unit with all the other triads in each stanza. Within each line a microcosmic linking is provided by the alliteration, which is generally in terms of two, though occasionally three, syllables.

The first three-line unit represents the topic statement, as it were, of the entire poem: "Lenten ys come with loue to toune, / With blosmen and with briddes roune, / That al this blisse bryngeth." Here are stated the subjects, themes, and images that permeate the rest of the poem—spring (*lenten*) and love, flowers (*blosmen*) and birds' song (*roune*), and bliss or joy. Also suggested is the relevance of these things to man in his own habitat, here seen as *toune*. At the

---

MS Harley 2253, fol. 71v, col. 1.
Index, no. 1861, p. 292; *Supplement*, p. 217.

Editions:
    Brown, *13*, no. 81, pp. 145–46.
    Chambers and Sidgwick, no. 5, pp. 8–9.
    Brook, no. 11, pp. 43–44.
    Sisam, pp. 164–65.
    Davies, no. 23, pp. 84–86.
    Stevick, *One*, no. 28, pp. 41–42.

Criticism:
    Wells, p. 494.
    Moore, pp. 53–54.
    Speirs, pp. 53–56.
    Manning, *CL*, pp. 231–33.

---

1. Brown, *13*, no. 52, pp. 101ff.

beginning of the poem the joy of life found in nature in the spring is seen to have come "to town," and the result must be concomitant happiness in man and a sense of his participation in life. But the rest of the first, as well as most of the second, stanza then describes the joy of spring and love in nature, not in man. It is only with line 23, at the end of the second stanza, that man, here the narrator, is brought explicitly into the poem. And, ironically, the narrator sees himself as one of the *mody* (23), that is, the moody or melancholy who cannot participate in this encompassing joy and love. The third stanza parallels the second in its development, and again at its end man is seen as being out of sorts with the rest of creation. If he cannot succeed in his love, he will, he says, leave human society and go live as a creature (*wyht*, 36) in the woods.

Each triad is end-stopped, a unit in its own right; and in each case there is a progression from the first and second lines, which generally parallel each other or at least make up a coordinate construction, to the third line, which acts as a culmination or working out of the first two lines. The first stanza contains a variety of patterns, but the one that becomes dominant in the poem may be seen in the second triad: "Dayeseyes in this dales, / Notes suete of nyhtegales, / Vch foul song singeth" (4–6). The first line here is joined by the second, and the thought, stemming particularly from the second line, continues into the third, which contains the main—or, as here, only—verb of the structure. This is also the pattern of lines 7–9, the next triad; and it is found generally throughout the second and third stanzas. The main variation on this pattern is the one seen in the first and last triads of stanza 1, based in each case on the subordination of the third line. In lines 10–12—"This foules singeth ferly fele, / And wlyteth on huere wynne wele, / That al the wode ryngeth"—the pattern is as follows: birds sing very much (10), and warble (11), so that the wood rings (12); but here the third line is still clearly the result of the first two.

In the initial triad the matter is more ambiguous. In line 3—"That al this blisse bryngeth"—*that* may mean "so that," but then *al* must be regarded as subject of *bryngeth* and *blisse* as its object; that is, the line would mean "So that everything brings this bliss." On the other hand, and more properly, *that* may refer to *blosmen* and *roune* (2), these being the things that bring bliss. But the poem lacks a definite ending for plural verbs in the present tense—using -*n*, -*s*, and -*th*, as in *waxen* (15), *wowes* (19), and *singeth* (10). A further, though less likely, possibility is that the ambiguous *that* may refer back to *lenten* (1)—though the *blosmen* and *briddes roune* are, along with *loue* (1), clearly to be identified with *lenten*. The ambiguity here seems most likely the result of an anacoluthon, and, indeed, varieties of anacoluthia mark most of the triads. Still, in each instance we are aware of the sense, even when it is not supported by an obvious grammatical structure.

All the details in the poem, aside from those about man, stem from the *blosmen* and the *briddes roune*, and all are likewise related to *loue*. The flowers provide the bulk of the visual details, and the birds' songs create the audial details. These songs are dominant in the first stanza where, except for the mention of daisies (4) and woodruff (9), all the details have to do with sound. Along with such nouns as *notes* (5) and *song* (6) are the verbs that describe and create sound: *singeth* (6, 10), *threteth* (complains, 7) *wlyteth* (warbles, 11), and *ryngeth* (12). In the second stanza, on the other hand, there is more of an even division between the two kinds of images. Those in the first six lines (13–18), showing the beauties of nature through its flowers, are visual; and those in the last six lines (19–24) are basically audial. These latter, however, do not have to do with song, as in the first stanza, but, rather, pertain to violence or dissatisfaction.

The first part of the third stanza is a blend of visual and audial imagery. Here the poet is concerned not with particular flowers and birds but with the natural forces of sunshine, moonlight, and dew; and in this setting we hear the sounds of birds and animals in general —*briddes* (27) and *deores* (29). But toward the end of this stanza, the narrator speaks of forgoing *this wunne weole* (35), "this wealth of joys," referring, it would seem, to the wealth of sights and sounds, as well as to the happiness implicit in them. And as the visual and audial images tend to leave the poem in this third stanza, the lyric may be seen as perfecting what appeared at the end of the second stanza when the narrator identified himself as one of the *mody* who are not in accord with love—"For loue that likes ille" (24)—or with nature. At the end of stanza 3, the contrast between the external world of nature and the internal feelings of the narrator is thus meanfully brought out. Or, to look at it in another way, the personification of nature that has been developing since the opening lines through the many sights and sounds breaks down as the narrator turns from the natural world, blotting it out, as it were.

The particular flowers and birds mentioned do more, however, than provide a certain kind of imagery. While some are doubtless included because of alliterative requirements, most may also be seen as particularly relevant to spring, life, and love, as well as to an innocence that marks this natural setting. The world of nature seen in this poem is like a prelapsarian world, and its bliss is of a purity not known in man's life or love. Nightingales (5) and thrushes (*threstel-coc*, 7) are the most popular of English song birds and, together with daisies (4), roses (13), and lilies of the valley (17), are traditional in medieval love literature. The red of the rose and the white of the lily (or lily of the valley), combining in the red and white of the English daisy, present colors traditionally seen as those of earthly love; and the birds listed here have similar associations. But the nightingale was also viewed, through its Latin name *luscina*, as signifying the light at the beginning of day,[2] the sense of newness and rejuvenation being reinforced in the poem by the lily of the valley and the daisy—here in the form of *dayeseyes*, "eyes of day"—both among the earliest flowers of the year.

These details also have pertinent religious connotations. The lily of the valley, in its whiteness and sweetness, was taken as a symbol of the Virgin Mary, especially of her Immaculate Conception.[3] The rose, noblest of flowers, was also associated with the Virgin, who was often termed "rose without thorn."[4] The combined medieval meanings of rose and lily of the valley—the lily itself was a traditional symbol of purity and of the Virgin[5]—stem from the passage in Canticles 2:1, "I am the rose of Sharon and the lily of the valley." The daisy, containing the red and white coloring of these two flowers, came to be used as a symbol of the Christ child in his innocence.[6] And in the way it appears in this poem—as *dayeseyes*—the flower is linked through catachresis to the eye of day or the sun. Moreover, the sun

---

2. Ambrose, *Hexaemeron*, v.xii.39 (*PL* 14:237–38); and Isidore of Seville, *Etymologiae*, xii.vii.37, ed. W. M. Lindsay, vol. 2 (Oxford, 1911).

3. On the lily of the valley as signifying the splendor of life eternal, see Bernard of Clairvaux, *On the Song of Songs* (London, 1952), p. 146. This flower was also seen as announcing spring and the coming of Christ: see A. P. de Mirimonde, "Fleurs et fruits du Paradis," *L'Oeil*, 156 (1967), 23.

4. Bartholomeus Anglicus, *De proprietatibus rerum*, xvii.136, trans. Stephen Batman, in *Batman upon Bartholome* (London, 1582), p. 659. See also Hugh of Saint Victor, *Sermo* lxv, "In nativitate Beatae Mariae" (*PL* 177:1104–05).

5. The lily was generally regarded, as Bartholomeus writes, as being "next to the Rose in worthiness and nobleness. . . . nothing is more gracious than the Lily in fairnes of colour, in sweetness of smell, and in effect of working and vertue" (*De proprietatibus rerum*, xvii.91, trans. Batman, pp. 629–30). See also Rabanus Maurus, *De universo*, xxii.viii (*PL* 111:528). *Mirk's Festial* associates the lily with the conception of Christ and tells a miracle of the Virgin where the lily is responsible for the conversion of Jews (ed. Theodor Erbe, EETS ES 96, London, 1905, 108–09).

6. Jacobus de Voragine, *Legenda Aurea*, cites St. Bernard's allegorization that Christ, "the Flower, willed to be born of a flower, in flower, and in the season of flowers" (trans. G. Ryan and H. Ripperger, London, 1941, 1:204).

(26) and the moon (25) also appear as attributes of Mary, having a source in Apocalypse 12:1, with its reference to the woman clothed with the sun, with the moon under her feet. It is not, however, that the poem is using these images to call up the Virgin Mary, or that what is here should be viewed as an allegory of her. Rather, this world is shown to be pure, and the purity is revealed through images traditionally associated with the Virgin.

The various flowers and herbs may also be seen as having medicinal qualities. According to medieval herbals, the daisy is good for healing broken bones, the rose for assuaging the fire of fever, and the lily of the valley for healing snakebites, swellings, and burns.[7] The herbs themselves detailed in the poem—woodruff (9), fennel (18), and chervil or wild thyme (*fille*, 18)—are even more potent remedies, though fennel and chervil were also viewed as being aphrodisiacs and consequently as enhancing lechery.[8] This may be the association that gives rise to the next lines in the poem that show animals making love—"Wowes this wilde drakes, / Miles murgeth huere makes" (19–20)—for the *wilde drakes* were notorious for the fury of their love-making.[9]

The only other particular animal reference is to *wormes* (31), which would seem distinctly out of place, in terms of both the other references and the idealized setting of the poem, for *wormes* (worms or snakes) are associated in the medieval bestiary tradition with destruction and death. According to the *Ubi sunt?* tradition, they are what is at the end of earthly love and happiness; but here, ironically, the "Wormes woweth vnder cloude" (31). Although Brown and other editors take *woweth* as an error for *waweth* (turns), and *cloude* as meaning "clod," that is, earth, it seems more likely that the *wormes* are "wooing under cloud." They are participating in the universal life and love, and, what is more, they seem to be above the ground—strange perhaps but certainly appropriate in a prelapsarian world. Joined in the triad with the *wormes* are women who, in a parallel statement, *waxeth wounder proude* (32)—somewhat like Eve in the Garden. Their activity is in one sense as incongruous as that of the *wormes*, for women, born from man's side, should be humble and be guided by the male. At the same time, the pride of women acts as a

---

7. See, e.g., *Agnus Castus, A Middle English Herbal*, ed. Gösta Brodin (Uppsala, 1950), pp. 147–48, 167–68, 200.

8. Ibid., pp. 157–58; *MED*, 3:487. Rabanus Maurus describes fennel allegorically as signifying the fragility of human nature (*De universo*, XXII.viii, *PL* 111:530).

9. See, e.g., Chaucer, *Parliament of Fowls*, l.360.

force negating the feelings of life and love. Their unnatural behavior is viewed as what keeps the narrator from participating in the *wunne weole* (35), and he seems to be condemning this behavior by putting it in a context marked by the wooing of *wormes*. Perhaps he is saying that even such monstrous and destructive creatures as *wormes* make love, but women will not. The forces of life and death would clearly seem to be reversed here.

Some words in the poem create problems. The last two words of line 11, "Ant wlyteth on huere wynne wele," reads in manuscript *wynter wele*, the exact opposite of what we would expect, and apparently represents an error resulting from a scribe's mistakenly re-copying *wynter* from line 8.[10] A different sort of problem is represented by "The mone mandeth hire bleo" (16). As the line stands, it makes enough sense; but there seems to be no justification for the mention of *mone* here and again in line 25—"The mone mandeth hire lyht." The term *mone* is different from the general expression *wynne wele*, and there is no need for it to be repeated, especially since none of the other particulars in the poem—rose, daisies, nightingales, etc.—is ever repeated. Moreover, there is little connection between line 16 and the next two lines of the triad—"The mone mandeth hire bleo, / The lilie is lossom to seo, / The fenyl and the fille" (16–18)—the order of which does not conform to any of the triad patterns seen earlier. Perhaps the whole line represents a scribal error, the copyist's eye slipping to line 25 which, except for the last word, duplicates this line. We should not, however, be upset with the repetition of *mandeth*, for it is common for verbs to be repeated in the course of this poem: *singeth* (6, 10, 27); *waxen, waxeth* (15, 32); and *wowes, woweth* (19, 31). Most likely, the problem has to do with the substantive *mone*. If it were read as *mont*, "hill," it could lead easily to the flowers of the next line that would cover it and give it its *bleo*, "color." *Mont* would also act to parallel *wode* in the previous triad and form a triad in the pattern of those found elsewhere in the poem. Another possibility is that *mone* should be *mond* (Latin *mundus*), although this is much less likely since the poem never makes such a general all-inclusive statement as would necessarily be made with a reference to "world." Rather, it stays with particulars, becoming slightly general only in the final stanza.

Line 20, "Miles murgeth huere makes," contains two difficulties. Whereas *miles* may be a Welsh word for "animals," Welsh loan words

---

10. *OED*, 12:2237; see also Brown, *13*, p. 230. Speirs, however, retains *wynter wele* on the grounds that it is intentionally ironic (p. 54).

are uncommon in Middle English, even though they are found elsewhere in poems in the Harley 2253 manuscript. Taking the word as
myles or *mules* does not improve matters, especially since mules are
neuter. In the same line, *murgeth* has frequently been translated as
"make merry," although with the next line—"As strem that striketh
stille"—the more precise meaning of this verb would seem to be
"merge," in the sense of "mate." The sound of the animals' coming
together would then, ironically but meaningfully, be seen resembling
the sound of "a stream that flows without moving" (*striketh stille*).

The use of paradox and anachronism is encountered throughout
the entire poem as the poet makes his language work to create a
general air of irony. As I read this lyric, it comes to exhibit, by the
middle of stanza 2, a tongue-in-cheek humor, the result of such
excesses and overstatements as the lovemaking of the *wilde drakes*
(19). This ironic note continues with the wooing of the *wormes*
(31), but it appears most clearly in the narrator's statements about
women and about his condition—even his final threat of being a
wyht in wode (36) seems like a humorous overstatement. Whereas so
many medieval poems take very seriously man's alienation from nature, this poem would seem to play with it and use the threat of it as
a means of seduction. But this attitude is within a description of nature that is essentially idealistic and without irony. Perhaps the narrator cannot take man seriously, but he certainly does respond to
nature, even when what he is presenting does not exist as such.

Wynter wakeneth al my care,
Nou this leues waxeth bare.
Oft y sike and mourne sare
4   When hit cometh in my thoht
Of this worldes ioie, hou hit geth al to noht.

Nou hit is, and nou hit nys,
Also hit ner nere ywys.
8   That moni mon seith, soth hit ys:
Al goth bote Godes wille;
Alle we shule deye, thah vs like ylle.

Al that grein me graueth grene,
12 Nou hit faleweth al bydene.
Ihesu, help that hit be sene
Ant shild vs from helle;
For y not whider y shal, ne hou longe her duelle!

MS Harley 2253, fol. 75v.

Index, no. 4177, p. 670; *Supplement*, p. 487.

Editions:

    Brown, *Rel 14*, no. 9, p. 10.

    Chambers and Sidgwick, no. 92, p. 169.

    Brook, no. 17, p. 53.

    Stevick, *One*, no. 30, p. 47.

Criticism:

    Wells, pp. 527–28.

    Reed, Edward Bliss, "Wynter Wakeneth Al My Care," *MLN*, 43 (1928), 81–84.

    Kane, p. 119.

    Speirs, pp. 58–59.

    Manning, *Wisdom*, pp. 105–06.

    Reiss, *AnM*, pp. 27–34.

BEGINNING AS A LAMENT about the coming of winter, the poem develops into an essay on mutability and concludes as a prayer for salvation. But the dominant theme in the three stanzas is the bewilderment that comes from the uncertainty of not knowing what the present holds and what the future will bring. It is a theme often expressed in medieval lyrics, frequently in a didactic but poignant statement, as in the following:

> Wanne i thenke thinges thre,
> Ne mai hi neuere blithe be:
> The ton is that i sal awei,
> The tother is i ne wot wilk dei,
> The thridde is mi moste kare—
> I ne wot wider i sal fare.[1]

In both poems the fact of mutability, the realization of the presence and imminence of death, is the initial concern, that which leads to further thought. And further thought makes man aware of his helplessness. In spite of his wishes to the contrary, he will die; and he will never know when. This combined certainty and uncertainty is bad enough, but even worse is not knowing the fate of one's soul after death. The *thinges thre* of this little poem are, like world, flesh, and devil, the ironic opposite of the usual groups of three in Christianity, which, like the Trinity and the theological virtues of hope, faith, and charity, stand for things of the spirit and act as inspirations for man. But here the *thinges thre* are such that they make man feel that he will *neuere blithe be*.

While this same thought appears in "Wynter wakeneth al my care," it is not presented in so orderly a manner, probably because this longer poem is doing more than stating the frightening facts of death and uncertainty. It illustrates them, presents them in metaphorical language, and uses them as the basis for a further action—the final prayer to Christ. In other words, the fact of man's helplessness pervades this poem, but the point of the poem is not to state this helplessness.

The first stanza begins with a comparison between man's feelings and winter weather; but ironically the line "Wynter wakeneth al my care" shows winter, a time when nature is sleeping, as it were, wakening feelings in man, although these feelings are of sorrow and therefore deadening to his spirit. *Wynter* and *wakeneth* are words not

---

1. Based mainly on the version in Arundel MS 292, fol. 3v; Brown, 13, no. 12B, p. 19; cf. Stevick, *One*, no. 21, p. 34.

ordinarily thought of in conjunction, but their association here through the /w/ alliteration leads to *care* which, while properly seen as linked to *wynter* in its suggestion of destructiveness, is also joined to *wakeneth* through the /k/ consonance and /a/ assonance. The entire stanza develops the relationship begun here and also creates a picture of the melancholy man. As in the first line, the verbs function ironically and paradoxically. To say that "Nou this leues waxeth bare" (2) is to use a verb of life and growth—like *wakeneth*—does not fit the action being described. And the linking of *waxeth* and *bare* through both grammar and assonance results in a strange coupling—comparable to that in the first line—which increases the sense of bewilderment. Moreover, with *waxeth* phonologically linked to *wakeneth*, and *care* to *bare*, a parallel situation is created, one giving the impression of cause and effect: when leaves become bare, then winter awakens the narrator's sorrow, though here the effect is stated before the cause. But *wynter*, seen literally, provides the setting and basis for line 2. In line 1, it functions metaphorically, calling up the winter, or old age, of life, becoming truly the winter of man's discontent and causing him to *sike and mourne sare* (3). These empty sounds and profitless tears are ironically what have flourished in his winter; they are the blossoms of the plant of melancholy or death that is his *care*.

Line 3 also introduces a series of clauses that, while stemming initially from the opening couplet about winter, tend to trail off into a musing of sorts as the narrator's *care* becomes more explicit. The first two lines have provided a setting that is now entered, as it were, and examined in detail. The sighs result from the narrator's concern about what happens to *this worldes ioie*, how the pleasures of this life *geth al to noht* (5). The *worldes ioie* is in one sense opposed to the narrator's *care* or lack of joy, although it is also like the *leues* (2) in that both *waxeth bare* and *geth al to noht*. Ironically, the only thing seen to grow here is man's sorrow about the process of dying which he sees all around him; and his *thoht* (4) becomes identified with, even the same as, his *care*. The verbs in these last three lines of the stanza support the irony, as did those in the first two lines. The narrator sighs and mourns (3) when it *cometh* (4) to his mind how everything *geth* (5) to nothing. It is this sense of coming and going that acts as the dominant point of the next stanza.

Picking up the *nou* of the first stanza (2), the second stanza begins with a reevaluation of the concept of time present. In line 2 *nou* functions to give a sense of immediacy to the narrator's frustration and sorrow. The winter he focuses on is occurring *nou*, a fact reinforced by all the verbs being in the present tense. But this sense of *nou*-ness is revealed as untrustworthy—"Nou hit is, and nou hit nys" (6)—so that exactly what is *nou* is moot, as is that which actually exists. The transitoriness seen as the present state in stanza 1 leads to the changeableness and insecurity of stanza 2. Nothing can be counted on as permanent, and when something is here one moment and gone the next, its reality must indeed be called into question. Thus line 7, "Also hit ner nere ywys"—meaning "As though it never were certain" (or "certainly")—may function as a culmination of the sense of coming and going. To be and then not to be is truly to appear unreal, to be seen as something that had never been (*ner nere*). There is another possible meaning in this line. Taking *ywys* to mean "certain" and re-evaluating grammatically *also* and *ner nere*, the line may then mean "Also it were not nearly certain." Although the first translation is the more likely, both reveal and emphasize the uncertainty of *hit*. While acting mainly as expletives, the three *hits* in lines 6–7 seem also to echo the same words in lines 4–5, referring to the realization that this world's joy *geth al to noht*. Syntactically, however, these earlier *hits*, especially that of line 5, refer in particular to *this worldes ioie*. And such would appear to be the meaning that provides the reference for the *hits* throughout the second stanza.

Line 8, "That moni mon seith, soth hit ys," continues the imprecise *hit*, now meaning the entire thought about worldly joy's coming to nothing; but it also changes the emphasis from the narrator's own response to that of others. Earlier we had seen the melancholy in his own mind (*in my thoht*, 4); but now he calls upon the words of *moni mon* to show that his own experience is to be viewed in the light of tradition and authority. This thought is what is *soth* and can be trusted. As such, it is different from the world and its joy, which can only deceive and frustrate. Furthermore, the words of authority, profitable sounds, as it were, here replace the sighs that had been the narrator's only voiced response (3). These take the form of the aphorism that "al goth bote Godes wille; / Alle we shule deye, thah vs like ylle" (9–10). The *al goth* echoes the *geth al to noht* of the concluding line of stanza 1, but here the verb means more explicitly "perishes" and leads to the exception of *Godes wille* that is not subject to mutability.

Whereas the precise meaning of *Godes wille* is somewhat ambiguous, it is clearly opposed to *worldes ioie* (5) and also to man who, like the leaves, *waxeth bare* (2). As the narrator says, "Alle we shule deye," the repeated *alle* emphasizing the point that everything shall perish that is not part of God or his will. Man has no say about life and death, even though *vs like ylle*. What is pleasing to man is seen to be nothing when compared to *Godes wille*. Whereas the first stanza was about the feelings of the individual narrator—he refers to *my care* (1) and *my thoht* (4)—the second stanza emphasizes mankind's response, the reactions of *moni mon* to the thought that *alle we shule deye*. The plurality is brought in to give additional force to the narrator's individual response and to contrast with God in his singularity and uniqueness—all of mankind cannot be compared in terms of power to *Godes wille*.

The emphasis on "all" is likewise seen at the beginning of the third stanza—in both lines 11 and 12—as is the repetition of *nou* (12), that has been a key word throughout the poem. "Al that grein me graueth grene, / Nou hit faleweth al bydene." This couplet, which may be based on the parable of the sower and the seed in John 12:24–25, involves a play on words more complicated and confusing than anything else in the poem. The initial *al* does not seem to fit grammatically into the line, but, following Brown and viewing the manuscript reading *gren* as *grein*, what comes after *al* may be translated as "All (that one buries, i.e.,) that grain that one buries green / Now it withers very quickly." The initial *al* may be seen in apposition to *that grein*, or rather, the *grein* is a metonomy for *al:* the seed at the source of life becomes dry and dead. If, however, *gren*—the original form—means "green," and *graueth* means "groweth," as some critics have thought,[2] the line would be read as "All that green (that) grows green for me." In any case, what is being detailed is a process from life to death; and the two *als* here reinforce the process of deterioration as they encompass apparently everything in the world, everything, that is, but Jesus, who can save man from his destruction, the *helle* (14) that awaits his sinful soul. Both *als* thus act as intensives, the second functioning to associate this word even further with destruction.

The movement is from *al my care* (1) and *al to noht* (5) through *al goth* (9), to *al bydene* (12), with various other uses of *al* as a substantive associated with destruction (10, 11). In each case this term of plurality is a pejorative, perhaps suggesting, as with *al bydene*, something excessive. As a substantive it functions like the pronoun-expletive *hit*, which in this stanza is revealed as synonymous with *al*, at least connotatively if not grammatically. The *al* that one *graueth* (11)—"buries" and "grows" here amount to the same thing—seems to be the same as the *hit* that *faleweth* (12). In fact, the construction *hit faleweth al* is identical with the earlier *hit geth al* (5)—where *al* may be functioning grammatically in two ways—and is related to the initial statement of the poem *Wynter wakeneth al*, where *wynter*, the sea-

---

2. See Reed, pp. 81–84, and Manning, *Wisdom*, pp. 105–6; also *MED*, 4: 337.

son of destruction, provides a basis for understanding the two noun substitutes.

The play on *gre(i)n* and *grene* in line 11 is clearly not accidental. Both terms suggest the same entity, which is youth or the beginning of life, but they function as nature images in terms of the *leues* that *waxeth bare* (2). With *gre(i)n* replacing *leues*, line 11 may be a restatement of this earlier image; or, as I prefer to read it, the earlier line may refer to one of the plants that have resulted from the growth of the "grain." But just as the leaves *waxeth bare*, so the grain *faleweth*. In this sense the movement is quickly (*bydene*) from the beginning of life to death, from *grene* to *bare*. Nothing of substance comes about—the theme of the second stanza—and it is no wonder that when the narrator calls on Jesus, who has here replaced the authority of *moni mon*, he asks him to "help that hit be sene" (13), the *hit* again referring to the same thing as the *al*, that which has been dying. The narrator asks that this be *sene*, literally "seen, visible," or more figuratively, "tangible or real." The implication is of real life as opposed to the shadowy, unreal, deceptive quasi-life that has been so frustrating to the narrator.[3] Along with this prayer for the real world, the narrator asks that mankind be saved—"shild vs from helle" (14)—most likely to be viewed here as the place of eternal *wynter* and *bare*-ness. Present also is the *vs* that had appeared in stanza 2, but now it joins the particular *y* and *me* representing the individual speaker.

The most noticeable feature of the poem has yet to be discussed: the long line at the end of each stanza, that climaxes the developing thought. Largely ametrical—although the lack of meter seems to become more pronounced from lines 5 and 10 to 15—these long lines provide what amounts to a denotative comment on the subject at hand. In the fourteenth century, prose was still the customary vehicle for serious writing—witness Chaucer's moral allegory in the *Melibee* and his sermon in the *Parson's Tale;* and pulpit oratory, the *ars praedicandi*, was ordinarily far apart from verse and its ornamentation. Furthermore, at the beginning of the Middle Ages Boethius had set an example for later centuries in the matter of alternating verse and prose, the *prosae* of his *Consolation of Philosophy* frequently being a denotative restatement of what had been said in his connotative *metra*. The difference between the two forms is something like De Quincey's distinction between the literature of knowledge and the literature of power, with power being understood as that which is emotionally effective. From St. Augustine to the Renaissance, the

---

3. In connection with this reading, *gre(i)n* may possibly be read as meaning trick or deceit, from OE *grin, gryn*. See *MED*, 4:376.

Christian justification for poetry was that it could convey powerfully the eternal verities, and that it could through its attractive veneer lead men to search for the truth within. The final long lines of his poem may be seen containing the truths of each stanza. Syntactically, they conclude the sentence that begins two lines before: whether independent clause or not, they function to give a clear statement of what is. Proverbial and aphoristic, these lines resemble Polonius's instructions; but here the context supports their truth. Also, in causing the stanzas to trail off into something they were not originally, these lines function as do the tail-rhyme stanzas of medieval romance. And if this poem were sung or accompanied by a musical instrument, the music would probably stop just before the last long line, which would then be recited as prose.

The first long line (5) is a dependent construction, being announced, at it were, by the line that comes before. But even apart from the other lines, though the *hou* is somewhat awkward, it makes sense: "Of this worldes ioie, hou hit geth al to noht." The second long line (10) presents a restatement of the concern in line 5 about everything's going to nought, with the application made specifically to man who will die and who is helpless about the matter: "Alle we shule deye, thah vs like ylle." The helplessness is a precondition for line 15, the third long line, where in an elliptical construction the narrator says, "For y not whider y shal, ne hou longe her duelle"—that is, "I do not know where I shall (go) or how long (I shall) dwell here." His concern is both with the journey after death and with the life before death, but the two conditions are strangely reversed. We might expect the concern about length of life to precede—structurally at least—the concern about the soul's final resting place. But as it stands, the end of the poem functions as a restatement of the fear of mutability seen in the other long lines, even though the certainty of death in line 10 is here replaced by the uncertainty about the time of its occurrence.

This clause, questioning the length of life, acts, moreover, as a return to the condition of this world and life as it is—the *wynter*, it would seem, that awakened the narrator's sorrow at the beginning of the poem. Also, the *ne hou* at the beginning of the second half of line 15—all three long lines are in two parts—echoes the *hou* of line 5; for the words *ne hou longe her duelle* is a restatement in reverse of the same thought in *hou hit geth al to noht*. A final point: the adverb *longe* in line 15 is something of an intentional anachronism, for everything associated with life has been seen as short. The word *longe* would more aptly refer to the soul's existence in *helle* (14); and, indeed, line 15, as it stands, might be read as "For I do not know where

I shall go, nor how long I shall dwell *there*." The *her* is unexpected and is likewise a reversal. As it may take the audience aback, at least momentarily, so it may help the return to the beginning of the poem.

Whereas these long lines tend to disrupt the structure and the smooth development of the poem, their being linked to the previous lines through syntax and rhyme keeps the disruption from being too serious. Furthermore, the first two long lines have a measured stress pattern—line 5 is iambic pentameter, and line 10 may best be read as tetrameter or hexameter. It is only with line 15, the longest of the three, that meter breaks down completely. Further counteracting the possible disruptive effects of these lines are the regular metrical pattern of the other lines—generally four-stressed, though lines 4, 9, and 14 may be regarded as three-stressed—and the regular *aaabb* rhyme scheme of each stanza. But the development is not in terms of the *a* triplet and the *b* couplet, with a pause between the two. Rather, after an initial couplet, the *a* rhyme continues as the first line of an *abb* triad, thus allowing the parts of the poem to be connected by final sounds. Linking occurs, moreover, through other sounds, especially those in such words as *al* and *hit* that appear throughout the stanzas, and those in various key words—the /w/, for instance, in *wynter*, *wakeneth*, *waxeth*, and *worldes* of stanza 1. Alliteration, assonance, and consonance are throughout very much a part of this poem and aid in making it one of the more interesting of the Middle English lyrics.

Wen the turuf is thi tuur,
And thi put is thi bour,
Thi wel and thi wite throte
4 Ssulen wormes to note—
Wat helpit the thenne
Al the worilde wnne?

Trinity Coll., Camb., MS 323, fol. 47v.
Index, no. 4044, p. 649; *Supplement*, p. 465.

Editions:
 Brown, *13*, no. 30, p. 54.
 Dickins and Wilson, p. 127.
 Stevick, *One*, no. 9, p. 12.

Criticism:
 Kane, p. 123.
 Dronke, *ML*, p. 69.
 Woolf, pp. 82–83.
 Oliver, p. 79.

In the late Middle Ages the pervasive contemplation of life's impermanence and death's invulnerability took all sorts of artistic and literary forms. Along with such dramatic motifs as the Dance of Death and the Debate between the Body and the Soul, there were also lyrical forms focusing on the question, "Ubi sunt qui ante nos fuerunt?" and on the refrain, "Timor mortis conturbat me." Frequently the "Sic transit mundi" theme took the form of something that may be called an "Ubi erunt?" theme. Best known today in English literature by its treatment in Andrew Marvell's "To His Coy Mistress," this theme directs the audience's attention to the question not of "Where are the snows of yesteryear?" but of what will happen to one's beauty, joy, and life in the future; and the future becomes as near as tomorrow. This "Ubi erunt?" question is one even more disturbing than the related "Ubi sunt?" theme because it concerns the future, not the past, that which is unknown and yet ahead for everyone, and because it deals with the mutability of the individual who is asking the question. The picture is a grim one of death's coming to the particular person, and lyrics asking such a question may be said to have a built-in effectiveness in that their question can hardly become trite. No one can quite answer the question, at least to his own satisfaction; and no one can avoid realizing that it is not an academic question.

The present lyric is in some ways a typical representative of this "Ubi erunt?" genre, but it is also one of the least overstated examples of the type. Frequently, such poems include a catalogue of various kinds of death and destruction; and, indeed, one could easily have been inserted here. It would have been possible after the first couplet, which talks about the grave as man's new home; and it might have been even more relevant following the second couplet, which describes briefly what will happen to the body after death. But instead of depending on such a list, this poem relies on understatement, indirectness, and a general calm though ironic detachment. These features, along with a direct address that implies an indirect threat to the reader, allow the lyric to make its point both concisely and effectively.

The poem is apparently based on six Latin lines which appear in the manuscript directly above the English text:

> Cum sit gleba tibi turris
> tuus puteus conclauis,
> pellis et guttur album
> erit cibus vermium.

Quid habent tunc de proprio
hii monarchie lucro?[1]

Even though the contents of the two poems are the same, the English version employs certain substantive and syntactic changes, as well as various rhythmical and alliterative devices, that make it more than a mere translation. In form it is an example of a "when-then" structure, a pattern very popular in medieval and Renaissance lyric poetry; but here the "when" clause seems to incorporate within itself a "then" clause that adds to its effectiveness. That is, the "when" clause would seem to be contained wholly within the first couplet, "Wen the turuf is thi tuur / And thi put is thi bour," being completed in the next two lines, "Thi wel and thi wite throte / Ssulen wormes to note." But because *thenne* is emphasized in the final couplet where the poem asks, or rather demands, "Wat helpit the thenne / Al the worilde wnne?" this couplet most likely represents the "then" clause that completes the thought projected in the first four lines of the poem. The real two-part division would thus appear to be after the implied "then" clause of the second couplet. Functioning both to complete the thought of the first couplet and to reinforce the "when" clause by showing in detail the fate of the body in the grave, this second couplet serves to culminate our understanding of the state of being that is referred to by the adverb substitute *thenne* in the final couplet.

The lyric begins with two transformations: the impersonal earth (*turuf*, 1) becomes man's dwelling and, even more significantly, his fortress (*tuur*). The irony is both that the resting place of man, that which is under the ground, should be referred to as a tower, something with which it would ordinarily be in contrast, and that the *turuf* is presented in the image of a fortress, protecting its inhabitants. As far as general sense is concerned, the second line—"And thi put is thi bour"—would seem only to repeat the condition of the first line; but it also emphasizes the irony by restating the image, along with making the even more striking transformation of the impersonal pit to the personal and safe bedroom (*bour*). Notwithstanding the spelling in manuscript, it seems most likely that *thi put* (2) parallels *the turuf* (1), and that the noun determiners in both represent the definite article "the."[2] These impersonal definite articles then contrast with

---

1. Quoted in Brown, p. 191. These lines are followed by the transitional *vnde anglice sic dicitur.*

2. The Latin is not really helpful on this point because, although its *tuus puteus* would support the "thy" reading, its next line, *pellis et guttur album,* shows no personal possessives comparable to those found in the English "*Thi*

the more personal possessive adjectives, "thy" of *thi tuur* (1) and *thi bour* (2), as the nouns themselves contrast. Both *tuur* and *bour* are images associated with the court and with the gay, carefree life, and lead to line 3—"Thi wel and thi wite throte"—with its emphasis on physical beauty. Similarly, the movement from the impersonal to the personal is significantly developed in the second couplet, where we find that the *wormes* will regard *thi wel* (skin) and *thi wite throte*. Both the possessive adjectives and the substantives here help to make the general question of the final two lines a particular and very personal one, demanding that we read line 5—"Wat helpit the thenne"—with an emphasis on *the*.

The second line of the poem also represents a development of the security suggested in line 1. The grave-fortress becomes the bed, but ironically one is not safe in it for, willy-nilly, the *wormes* will get in. The inverted syntax of lines 3–4, "Thi wel and thi wite throte / Ssulen wormes to note," enables the poem to continue the emphasis on "thy" as well as to reinforce with the paralleled *wel* and *wite throte* the kind of linking found earlier in *turuf-tuur* and *put-bour*. The inversion also allows the shocking information about the worms to come at the end of the thought. We focus on skin and throat but do not realize until we have finished line 4 that they are the object of the sentence. What they in their helpless state will be subjected to is not stated: the infinitive *to note* (observe, regard) disguises the imminent action but yet suggests in its understatement and euphemism more horrors than a more explicit verbal would call up.[3]

A similar inverted syntax appears in the last question, where the key infinitive *wnne* is placed at the end: "Wat helpit the thenne / Al the worilde wnne?" (5–6). This inversion ironically emphasizes the loss that is being described and that will really exist someday for all people. Also, *the worilde*, paralleling *the turuf* and *thi put*, is given a connotation quite different from what it usually has; for the man who is in the grave may be said in one sense to have gained (*wnne*) the world. It might be queried whether the last line as presented here, "Al the worilde wnne," represents the best reading. Even though the interpretation of *worilde wnne* as weak adjective plus noun, meaning "wordly joy," is supported by the Latin *monarchie lucro*, the form *worilde* with its three syllables is unusual. What seems to be the implied and even the demanded reading is something like *world to*

---

wel and *thi* wite throte." The English poet is clearly not following the Latin in its use of definite articles and possessive adjectives.

3. Woolf, however, glosses *note* as "benefit" (p. 82).

wnne.[4] The infinitive *to wnne* would then clearly parallel the earlier *to note* (4), as it seems meant to, contrasting the active striving of men for wordly pleasure with the rather impassive but finally overwhelming "noting" of the conqueror worm. Without even trying, the worms will prevail, and man's attempts are ironically shown to be futile. Furthermore, man's striving to progress and succeed provides no help (5) for himself at the end of his life: such activity will not keep the worms from him and will not prevent the devils, often symbolized by *wormes*, from taking his soul. The implied ideal is for man to have a final resting place—*tuur* and *bour*—that is not *turuf* and *put*, but heaven, frequently seen as a tower. If one is not really in the earth, there will be no horror and no final destruction by the *wormes*.

It is relevant that the reading in the Latin describing the fate of the body is in at least one point quite different from the English. Whereas in the Latin the flesh and white throat are seen as food for worms—"pellis et guttur album / erit cibus vermium"—in the poem at hand the infinitive *to note* is used to describe the action of the *wormes*. It is clear that the English poem is concerned with dramatically presenting the fate of the body, not merely with stating the fact of physical decomposition. But the verbal, *to note*, interesting as it is, may represent a scribal error. Throughout the poem the principle governing the sounds has been the alliteration of two stresses in each line, either fully—as in *turuf-tuur* (1) and *wel-wite* (3)—or nearly, *put-bour* (2), where the voiceless bilabial stop /p/ is echoed by its voiced counterpart /b/. But this principle is not continued in line 4, where *wormes* and *note* are the stressed syllables. Even though the assonance and nasal consonance that are present may seem sufficient, it is possible that *note* should be read as *uote*, that is, *wote* (OE *witan*). As such it would mean "know" or "be familiar with," essentially the same as the "observe" meaning of *note*. But as *wote*, it might also be related to OE *witan* and mean "guard, defend, keep safe."[5] Such a meaning would represent an ironic continuation of the emphasis on safety and security found in the first two lines with *tuur* and *bour*. At the same time, it is clear how the *wormes*, as "guardians" of the grave, would defend the dead person's *wel* and *wite throte*.

The word *throte*—Latin *guttar*—may be especially functional here. Line 3, describing "Thi wel and thi throte," may be seen as moving from the general, the *wel* (flesh), to the particular, the *wite throte*; but we might wonder why this specific particular. Besides suggesting

---

4. Of modern editors, Stevick is apparently alone in translating the phrase as "to win the world" (*One*, p. 12).

5. Cf. *wite*, v2 in *OED*, 12:209, and *wittie*, v2 in *OED*, 12:229.

the courtly, the sensuous, and the vulnerable, the throat was frequently seen in the exegetical tradition as a symbol for the grave, as
in Psalms 5:11, echoed in Romans 3:13: "Their throat is an open
sepulchre." The throat was also a symbol of gluttony, as may be seen
for instance in the writings of St. Augustine and Rabanus Maurus;[6]
and one form of gluttony was the accumulating of possessions. The
white throat may thus function as both an ironic reference to the
grave and a transition to the question of the last couplet, which relates the death and destruction seen in the first four lines to those
specifically concerned with *wnne* (gain). As is clear throughout
medieval literature the "winner" is no better than the "waster"; each
is a state of excess, and each represents a perversion of the ideal of
moderation.[7] It is a fitting punishment for those concerned with gain-
ing the world to be wasted by it, and, further, for the world to become finally the *turuf*, of which the dead body clearly has a surfeit.

The detached irony of the final question in this lyric keeps the
didacticism implicit. But the question is really a rhetorical one—of
erotesis (*interrogatio*)—that cannot be answered. The silence that
must follow it acts as the final line of the poem, and during this silence the general audience, as well as the particular *the* (5) to whom
the poem is addressed, makes the specific application to itself.

---

6. Augustine, *Confessionum*, x.xxxi.47 (*PL* 32:799); Rabanus Maurus, *De Universo*, vi.1 (*PL* 111:156–57).

7. Cf. the Middle English *Winner and Waster*.

Wanne mine eyhnen misten,
And mine heren sissen,
And mi nose koldet,
4 And mi tunge foldet,
And mi rude slaket,
And mine lippes blaken,
And mi muth grennet,
8 And mi spotel rennet,
And min her riset,
And min herte griset
And mine honden biuien,
12 And mine fet stiuien—
Al to late, al to late,
Wanne the bere ys ate gate!

Thanne y schel flutte
16 From bedde to flore,
From flore to here,
From here to bere,
From bere to putte—
20 And te putt fordut.
Thanne lyd min hus vppe min nose;
Off al this world ne gyffe ihic a pese.

Trinity Coll., Camb., MS 43, fol. 73v.
Index, no. 3998, p. 640; *Supplement*, p. 458.

Editions:
  Brown, *13*, no. 71, p. 130.
  Davies, no. 17, pp. 74–75.

Criticism:
  Malone, Kemp, "Notes on Middle English Lyrics," *ELH*, 2 (1935), 58–65.
  Kane, p. 121.
  Manning, *Wisdom*, pp. 15–17.

ON THE GENERAL SUBJECT of the contemplation of death, this poem is in some ways very similar to the previous lyric, "Wen the turuf is thi tuur," although this much longer piece falls more particularly within the genre of the metrical catalogue listing the signs of death, the *proprietates mortis*. More meaningful, though less immediately striking, is the difference in points of view of the two poems. Whereas the previous lyric was homiletic in nature, being directed at a "thee," this piece, told in the first person, makes use of a narrator who reports his condition at the moment, as it were, of his own death.

Again there is a "when-then" construction, although both sections are much more detailed and developed than in the former poem. The lengthy "when" clause here provides a developing picture of the coming of death, and even though the list of signs from the misty eyes (1) to the stiffening feet (12) are parallel, there is a sense of movement from life to death. But the catalogue is exaggerated, perhaps intentionally so, to create, instead of a real feeling of horror, a sense of the melodramatic and the grotesque. The anaphora created by *And mi(ne)* leads to a series of coordinated dependent clauses which are too pronounced and vivid in their details to be realistic. Furthermore, the homely imagery—for instance, the nose getting cold (3), the spittle running out of the mouth (8), the hair standing on end (or perhaps falling out, 9)[1]—along with the end-stopped rhymed couplets, creates the impression of a ridiculous death. The picture given may well be an accurate reflection of what is in store for all men, but it is the ludicrousness, not the fear, of such an end that prevails. Here the dying man is not horrible, tragic, or sad; he is only ridiculous, even laughable; and few of us can visualize such a condition as the proper end of life.

Lines 13–14, "Al to late, al to late, /Wanne the bere ys ate gate!" represent in one sense a culmination of the "when" clause. That is, when the signs appearing in lines 1–12 are seen, it is too late for man to do anything about them or about his physical condition. But syntactically, the repeated "al to late" (13) is not the beginning of a "then" clause. Rather, this phrase tends to break into the catalogue, evoking the significance of the signs. Referring to the approach of the bier, these lines represent both another result of the signs and a referral back of sorts. When the eyes mist and the other things happen, we then realize that these are signs that the bier is imminent and that at this time it is too late. But, we might wonder, too late for what? The only clear answer is that it is too late to live further. And as lines

1. See Malone, p. 64, and Davies, p. 315.

1–12 detail the signs of death, so lines 15–20, in the form of the awaited "then" clause, detail the imminent movement of the body to the grave.

The *I* is still the focal point and main actor and, as the narrator moves from bed to floor, to shroud, to bier, to grave, we go from the known, familiar, and casual to the unknown, strange, and hostile. With line 20—"And te putt fordut"—the motion begun with *misten* and *sissen* (1–2)[2] and continuing with the projected floating or carrying (*flutte*, 15),[3] stops abruptly as the grave is closed up (*fordut*), representing the cessation of all life. At this point, with the second "then" clause—"Thanne lyd min hus vppe min nose" (21)—the ludicrous element in the poem is clear, even though this homely line may be a direct translation of a line from a Latin hymn, perhaps in the form of "Quando domi summitas super nasum iacet."[4]

But these two "when" clauses and two accompanying "then" clauses concern only the action itself, not its explicit meaning or significance. It is with the last line of the poem—"Off al this world ne gyffe ihic a pese"—that we get the result of the action and the individual's response to it. Throughout the preceding twenty lines the rhythm has been in the form of two stresses per line, in the first paragraph generally in the form of an anapest followed by an amphibrach —XX/|X/X—and in the second paragraph in the form of two amphibrachs—X/X|X/X—or perhaps two iambs, depending on how forcefully the final schwa sounds are to be pronounced. With line 20, however—"And te putt fordut"—this rhythm ends; and in the masculine ending *fordut*, contrasting with the feminine endings of the preceding lines, we can almost hear the shutting of the coffin as well as the closing up of the grave. Line 21—"Thanne lyd min hus vppe min nose"—inaugurates a new rhythm, a regular iambic tetrameter, that resembles, in effect at least, the two tetrameters at the end of the first paragraph—"Al to late, al to late, / Wanne the bere ys ate gate" (13–14). But then all rhythm breaks down in the prosaic statement and contemplative imprecation of the final line. With "Off al this world ne gyffe ihic a pese," the speaker shows his disgust at such an end. Here is the final grotesquerie of the poem and the triumph of the

---

2. The words *heren sissen* have been taken by some editors to mean "ears are full of hissing" (e.g., Davies, p. 74), but more likely they mean "ears (or hearing) cease."

3. Malone (p. 63) points out that while *flutte* generally means "go," it is used here more in the sense of "be carried" (from ON *flytja*).

4. Dreves, 33:262; cited in Davies, p. 315.

homely. An incongruous response to the situation of death, it shows the narrator's ultimate scorn of the waste of it all.

We may see the effectiveness of such an ending by comparing this final line with the moral statement given in a late fourteenth-century English lyric that according to Brown is evidently an amplification of this culminating judgment. Part of it reads as follows:

> Sore the shal rewe
> Old synnes and newe,
> That thou noldest wepen
> And thi synnes leten,
> Whanne thou shalt underfon
> Aftir thou hast here don.[5]

This is the customary homily we might expect at the conclusion of such dramatized statements of death. These and similar words tell the audience to observe, understand, and change its ways so that it can avoid so grotesque an end. It would seem that by being saved, man is consequently less vulnerable to the ludicrous. Such moralizing, however, represents an overstatement; it is not needed, and it changes the tone of the entire poem. Keeping the homely and ludicrous, on the other hand, allows for misanthropy and satire, and, thereby, the effective working out of medieval horror. To understand this, we should realize that the grotesque represented for the Middle Ages a perversion of the ideal. To oversimplify, the good was beautiful and the bad was ugly; and that which is ugly is laughable. But the laughter that one would direct at the ugly is raucous not pleasant, and very different from, say, a subdued smile or any expression of joy or internal harmony. When laughter is directed at something, it is obviously different from a joyful or cheerful response to that which is considered wonderful.

In the present lyric man is presented as a victim, as someone helpless and hopeless. And the speaker, who stands for mankind, is, with his homely language, little better than a clown. At the same time, even though his response as expressed in the last line is inadequate, it acts as an indication of the right view of life, here the contempt of things of this world, which would presumably allow man to avoid such an end. Everything in this poem implies that man is crude, ugly, without any nobility or real worth, at least insofar as his physical existence is concerned. The end shown in the poem is necessarily

---

5. See Brown, 13, p. 221; based on Bodl. MS 416, fol. 109.

that of those who care too much about *temporalia*, who give to the world more than a *pese*.[6] This is the view of life ordinarily described as *contemptus mundi*, although in this poem *contemptus hominis* might be a more appropriate term. Still, although the moralizing may be implicit, even imminent, it is its lack, as well as the plain language used, that makes this piece compelling and effective today. As George Kane writes, "While it is hardly possible to like this lyric one is compelled to admire it and to concede that its author has powerfully concentrated in it the raw material of the harrowing sermon."[7]

---

6. Although in the proverbial expression of not giving a pea, the pea is clearly worth little, in Christian iconography it sometimes symbolizes fertility. See, e.g., *The Hours of Catherine of Cleves*, intro. and comm. John Plummer (New York, n.d.), pl. 3 and note, where singing angels are shown with a border of peas in open pods in a setting that was probably part of the Annunciation to Saint Anne. If applicable in this poem, such fertility would exist as the ironic opposite of the sterility and death dwelt upon in detail.

7. Kane, p. 121. In relation to this and other lyrics on death, see Woolf's chapter on the subject, pp. 67–113.

Wel, qwa sal thir hornes blau,
Haly Rod thi day?
Nou is he dede and lies law
Was wont to blaw thaim ay.

Lansdowne MS 207, fol. 434.
Index, no. 3894, p. 624; *Supplement,* no. 3857.5, p. 438.

Editions:
Dickins and Wilson, p. 118.
Stevick, *One,* no. 23, p. 35.

Criticism:
Wilson, *Early,* p. 273.
Wilson, *Lost,* p. 187.
Reiss, *CE,* 27 (1966), 377–79.
Robbins, R. H., "A Highly Critical Approach to the Middle English Lyric,"
CE, 30 (1968), 74–75.
Reiss, "Concerning Literary Meaning," *CE,* 30 (1968), 76–78.

NEGLECTED IN THE STANDARD COLLECTIONS of Middle English lyrics, this poem deserves to be better known than it is. Apparently originating in the late thirteenth century as a lament for the death of Lord Robert de Neville, whose men, despite the Church's antagonism, used to blow their horns to celebrate the slaying and sacrifice of a stag,[1] the poem has come to have much more meaning than this historical association would indicate. At least it may be said of the version printed here that it has transformed the local and trivial into something universal and significant, having relevance to those who never heard of Lord Neville. To say that the statement of historical fact is the same as the poem, or to confuse the efficient cause of a work of literature with the work's meaning, is to mishandle and misunderstand this poem in particular and literature in general. No matter what the lyric may have meant in its earliest form, the version here has little or nothing to do with the local and particular events that caused it to come into being.[2]

In the form of simple ballad meter, this poem may even contain, as Wilson thinks, "the authentic note of the ballad, appearing long before the earliest written examples."[3] Be this as it may—the thirteenth-century poem "Judas" is another seen as both ballad and lyric—we may still note that a narrative is the basis of the poem. That is, an action has been completed before the poem begins; we enter not *in medias res* but *post res*. The poet is not interested in telling us the story of this action, unless, as Wilson believes, these four lines represent a "single stanza of a lost Middle English ballad"[4]—a point I shall not argue here, for I hope to show that the poem is sufficiently self-contained to be in no need of additional stanzas.

Although the lyric opens with a question, a device frequently used as an easy way of injecting drama into a poem, the opening here seems almost casual, even unconcerned, an effect due to the use of the expletive *wel* as the first word, and to the innocence of the question, "who shall blow these horns." Hardly the "lo!" often used at the beginning of heroic narratives, *wel* seems strikingly nonheroic, even familiar. But innocent as these lines may at first appear, they gain in power and meaning as the last two lines reveal the reason for the question. The answer to the question, we may note, is still not given; and in this lack of solution lies part of the poem's interest. It asks a

1. Robbins, *CE*, p. 75.
2. See Reiss, *CE*, 30 (1968), 76–78.
3. Wilson, *Early*, p. 273.
4. Wilson, *Lost*, p. 187.

question that we cannot easily answer and be done with. It makes us face the problem of the death, as stated in line 3, and see its absurdity.

Another manuscript reading of the first line, however, provides some complications: "Wel and wa sal ys hornes blawe."[5] Here instead of a question is a *wellaway*, which apparently acts as a Northern type of pibroch given, according to Robbins, by the retainers of Lord Neville for their deceased feudal lord.[6] But whereas this reading may explain what was once behind the line, it is not necessarily superior to the "Wel, qwa sal thir hornes blau" found in the version under discussion. What is clear is that in each case the line introduces a different poem having a particular theme if its own. Whether or not the "Wel, qwa sal" reading was the result of an error, the poet who formed this first line as a question had a point of his own different from that of the other poet.

As the poem exists in the version given here, its main point is not to lament the death of a town's horn blower, him who used to blow the horns at the Feast of the Holy Cross on September 14. Rather, the focus is on the irony and incongruity resulting from the juxtaposition of the joy of this feast, celebrating the return of the cross to Jerusalem, and the poignant sorrow of the horn blower's death—something also seen in the "Wel and wa" version. There is, moreover, an implicit contrast between Christ who, raised on a cross, rose up alive and the man here who is "dede and lies law" (3). The last line—describing him who was *wont* (accustomed) to blow the horns *ay* (always)—places the emphasis on the permanent and contrasts, again ironically, with the *nou* of line 3 and with the immediate fact of the death. The result is to make us intensely aware of this death and of how it occurs in a context of eternity. No matter what the poem may originally have meant, the version here is far from Lord Neville and his retainers. It has transcended local interest and now has a significance for all mankind, as may be demonstrated by the existence of various versions of this lyric, extant even in the nineteenth century.

The four lines, to be sure, act as a eulogy for the dead horn blower—he was unique, he was a necessary member of the community, he will not be replaced easily—and the horns sound for him as well as for Holy Cross Day. Perhaps, at the same time, there is a suggestion of hope. Just as Christ rose, so may this man. There may be a further parallel with the cross, which was figuratively "laid low," then discovered buried in the ground, and raised up by St. Helena. Also, ac-

5. Lansdowne MS 207, fol. 434; cited in Robbins, *CE*, p. 74.
6. Robbins, *CE*, p. 75.

cording to legend, the cross was able to renew itself whenever part
of its wood was removed, living on, as it were. But, to repeat, the
main emphasis is on the moment, on the *nou*, and now there is little
of anything but grief.

As it stands, this poem may be viewed as an exclamation of personal sorrow, but the sorrow is seen in a larger context. The past—
the crucifixion and the history of the cross—and the future—if the
blowing of horns here acts as a suggestion of Judgment Day—come to
bear on the moment at hand. They give a meaning to the mortality,
of which we are so vividly made aware; instead of denying the fact or
the sadness of this mortality, they contrast with it. A further element
that should be considered is the meaning of *thi* in line 2. Is it merely
a definite article, does it mean "this," or should it be translated as
"thy," referring back to *Haly Rod?* If "thy" were its meaning, the
question would then read, "Who will blow these horns, Holy Cross,
on thy day?" and would be a direct address to the Cross, perhaps
even a prayer or invocation for help—this, it should be emphasized,
in spite of what the poem may originally have meant.

In its structure the lyric is very much like that well-known poem
from the early sixteenth century:

> Westron winde, when will thou blow,
> The smalle raine downe can rain?
> Christ, if my love were in my armes,
> And I in my bed again![7]

Here again we see ballad meter and the suggestion of a narrative;
here again we have a question-answer pattern, and again the answer
is really no solution but a comment that allows the opening lines to
be far more powerful and suggestive than we would at first think.
But "Westron winde" has an agonizing cry that makes its tone very
different from the earlier poem, where much of the effectiveness lies
in the restraint of its final lines.

---

7. See, e.g., the text printed in *Poetry of the English Renaissance, 1509–
1660*, ed. J. W. Hebel and H. H. Hudson (New York, 1929), p. 42.

Maiden in the mor lay,
   In the mor lay;
Seuenyst fulle,
4   Seuenist fulle;
Maiden in the mor lay,
   In the mor lay,
Seuenistes fulle ant a day.

8 Welle was hire mete.
   Wat was hire mete?
The primerole ant the—
   The primerole ant the—
12 Welle was hire mete.
   Wat was hire mete?
The primerole ant the violet.

Welle was hire dryng.
16   Wat was hire dryng?
The chelde water of the—
   The chelde water of the—
Welle was hire dryng.
20   Wat was hire dryng?
The chelde water of the welle-spring.

Welle was hire bour.
   Wat was hire bour?
24 The rede rose an te—
   The rede rose an te—
Welle was hire bour.
   Wat was hire bour?
28 The rede rose an te lilie flour.

A FREQUENTLY CITED Middle English lyric, this poem has especially been singled out for analysis by those interested in understanding and demonstrating the symbolic nature of medieval literature and in seeing how an ostensibly secular work is essentially and actually religious.[1] But even though it has been a focal point for discussions about the validity of the exegetical approach to literature, it still needs to be treated fully for itself, to see further how it is, in Edith Sitwell's phrase, "a miracle of poetry."[2] The method of the poet here is to approach his subject obliquely. Using language that appears to be innocuous, he refers indirectly to what is his real subject; and, moreover, he fragments the thought of the poem, thereby asking the audience to examine in detail what is being presented. Instead of a narrative, the poem gives a picture, a static pageant that reveals particular details of the scene before us. But also, as the four stanzas progress, we tend to feel that we are learning more about the *maiden* as the questions concerning her are answered. These answers, how-

---

Bodl. MS 13679 (formerly Rawlinson D. 913), item 1 (h); written as prose;
    second and third stanzas expanded following Sisam.
Index, no. 3891, p. 623; *Supplement*, no. 2037.5, p. 238.

Editions:
    Robbins, *Sec.* no. 18, pp. 12–13.
    Sisam, p. 167.
    Davies, no. 33, p. 102.
    Stevick, *One*, no. 38, pp. 60–61.

Criticism:
    Wells, p. 493.
    Robertson, D. W., Jr., "Historical Criticism," in *English Institute Essays 1950*, ed. Alan S. Downer (New York, 1951), pp. 26–27.
    Tillyard, E. M. W., *TLS*, 50, May 11, 1951, 293.
    Schoeck, R. J., *TLS*, 50, June 8, 1951, 357.
    Greene, Richard L., " 'The Maid of the Moor' in the *Red Book of Ossory*," *Speculum*, 27 (1952), 504–06.
    Speirs, pp. 62–64.
    Donaldson, E. T., "Patristic Exegesis in the Criticism of Medieval Literature: The Opposition," in *Critical Approaches to Medieval Literature,* ed. Dorothy Bethurum (New York, 1960), pp. 21–24.
    Manzalaoui, Mahmoud, "*Maiden in the Mor Lay* and the Apocrypha," *N&Q*, 210 (1965), 91–92.
    Dronke, *ML*, pp. 195–96.

---

1. See Schoeck, p. 357, Robertson, pp. 26–27, and in opposition, Greene, *Speculum*, pp. 504–06, and Donaldson, pp. 21–24.
2. *A Poet's Notebook* (Boston, 1950), p. 245.

ever, are ambiguous or, rather, paradoxical and not very meaningful unless we are aware of their symbolic significance.

The first stanza presents the situation, but it is one that we cannot immediately comprehend. It is not within our usual experience to be presented with a maiden who lay on a moor, much less with one who lay there more than seven nights. We have begun *in mediis rebus,* and we may properly expect the rest of the poem to make meaningful what has gone before, who the maiden is, and why she stayed on the moor for so long a time. This the poem does only partly, for each of the subsequent three stanzas examines an aspect of this situation. It is thus a given or norm, and what follows depends on its existence. Whether or not we understand the situation, we have to accept it and proceed from it. The next stanzas also continue to create paradoxes, as all three insist how *welle* she was cared for on the moor: stanza 2 states that she fed on primerole and violet, stanza 3 that she had cold spring water to drink, and stanza 4 that she rested on roses and lilies. Matters have hardly been cleared up by these explanations. The details themselves have not caused the situation of the poem to become meaningful. Unless we wish to claim that the poem as it exists is really unfinished and corrupt, or that it is playful gibberish in an Edward Lear vein, we must understand the signification of the details that are the only givens we have.

The maiden lying on the moor is certainly a helpless creature, but she is also one who has apparently been singled out for special actions and special care. In the middle of a moor—ordinarily to be thought of as a wild, dangerous, inhospitable place—she reclines on flowers and is nourished by comforting Nature. This maiden must be a special creature. Our first reaction may be that she is a courtly lady in a bower of bliss, or perhaps "a kind of water-sprite living in the moors";[3] but all the imagery of the poem supports her further identification as the Virgin Mary. The primerole and violet (stanza 2) are symbols of her simplicity and humility, the cool water (stanza 3) suggests her cleanness and God's grace, and the rose and lily (stanza 4) act to signify her charity and purity.[4] As these objects function on the sur-

---

3. As argued by Dronke, *ML,* p. 195.

4. Louis Réau, *Iconographie de l'art chrétien* (Paris, 1955), 1:133; and Robertson, p. 27. Tillyard (p. 293), going in the right direction, would have the maiden be an ascetic, like the penitent Mary Magdalene who, in *Piers Plowman,* is described as having "by mores lyved and dewes" (B. xv.288–89). In the C version (xviii, 2122), the Magdalene is joined by Mary of Egypt. Schoeck (p. 357) would have the maiden be any member of the Church who is of pure faith, though Speirs (p. 63) thinks of the maiden as perhaps a vestal or as someone undergoing a rite of maturation or purification. For Manzalaoui (p.

face of the poem, they are not literally aspects of Mary but, rather, things given to her. Even so, they are shown to be associated with her, and the association has point because of her role as the mother of Christ.

As Robertson points out, the moor represents the world before Christ, a barren place where homeless man can survive only through miraculous intervention.[5] Creation—that is, postlapsarian creation—would necessarily be a barren place without Christ's existence, at least in contrast to what it would be like after his birth. And perhaps we are seeing Mary waiting the full seven days—here seven nights—until it is time for the birth of Christ, which would be on the eighth night. It is doubtful that the poet is making a common day-night contrast here, for "se'night" is a customary Middle English form for seven days, as is "fortnight" for fourteen days. But still the choice of "night" may be significant, first, in suggesting further the dangers of the maiden's existence on the moor, and, second, in leading by contrast to the great day that came with Christ and that will come at the end of the world. In another sense, the moor and the seven nights suggest the labor of Mary before the birth of her son. She is away from the world in the wilderness—as Christ is to be before he begins to fulfill his role in this world; but her labor is not presented as a time of pain. She is God's special servant and agent, and all of creation serves her. Furthermore, the springtime of the world seems to be at hand: the *primerole* (from Latin *primula*, diminutive of *primus*) probably here refers to a daisy or cowslip, both early spring flowers, as is the *violet* (14). The *chelde water* is from the *welle-spring* (21), a traditional source of life; and, indeed, from Mary will come the personification of eternal life.[6]

Primerole, violet, and fresh water, along with rose and lily, are all out of place on a moor and suggest, on the other hand, a garden both luxuriant and ever fresh and new. But this is a garden like Spenser's Garden of Adonis (*FQ*, III) which is the source of life and from

---

92), who sees an echo of 2 Esdras, 9, both Esdras and the Maiden "are types of the soul in expectancy, in a stage of purification prior to the vision of Divine Truth." Joseph Harris, in a forthcoming article in the *Journal of Medieval and Renaissance Studies*, demonstrates that a ballad tradition of the Magdalene's penance is the basis of this poem, and that the imagery suggests that the subject here is both the Magdalene and the Virgin.

5. Robertson, p. 27.

6. On the Virgin as the well of living waters, see, e.g., Bernard of Clairvaux, "Sermo in nativitate B. V. Mariae," 2 (*PL* 183:439). Schoeck thinks of the *chelde water* as the "*Christus irrigans* or the Holy Spirit, or true doctrine or baptism," and the *seuenist fulle* as "the seven sacraments" (p. 357).

which comes the force of *Natura naturans* that drives and invigorates the natural world. It is not a false Bower of Bliss (*FQ*, II) or a Garden of Deduit or sensual delight, as in the *Roman de la Rose* and its tradition, even though the terminology is appropriate to writings associated with courtly love. The end of this "garden" is rejuvenation and revitalization, and Mary's fruit, Christ, will bring new life to the world.[7]

Technically, the poem supports and reinforces its symbolic significance. As I view the four stanzas, they are each in seven lines, though there is a problem about the structure because in manuscript the piece is written as prose, with what are here the third and fourth stanzas presented in an abbreviated form. Still, the number of lines in each stanza—seven—seems significant; and Robbins is surely wrong when he prints lines 3–4 as one line, thereby causing the first stanza to contain six lines. The "seven" restates structurally the only number mentioned in the poem—in *seuenist*—and emphasizes its importance. In medieval number symbolism seven was traditionally the number of completeness or totality, and more specifically of the seven ages of the world.[8] What follows seven—here the *ant a day* (7)—is regeneration, immortality, the day of rebirth, or the beginning of eternity following mutability.[9] In the traditional medieval view seven was seen as composed of four and three. Four, signifying things earthly or mundane,[10] as opposed to three which stood for things spiritual, is additionally revelant here in that the poem is composed of four stanzas. Furthermore, the combination of four and seven producing twenty-eight—the total number of lines in this poem—is likewise significant; for this number, being the sum of the numbers one through seven, was viewed in neo-Pythagorean thought as a perfect number.[11] We might also expect the number of stresses in each line to contribute to the number symbolism that seems to be operating in this lyric, but these stresses lack regularity. It would seem that in each stanza all lines except the last are two-stressed, but the last line—

7. See, e.g., D. W. Robertson, Jr., "The Doctrine of Charity in Mediaeval Literary Gardens: A Topical Approach through Symbolism and Allegory," *Speculum*, 26 (1951), 24–49.

8. See, e.g., Augustine, *De civitate Dei*, xx.5 (*PL* 41:663).

9. See esp. Augustine, *Contra Faustum Manichaeum*, xvi.29 (*PL* 42:335–36); Hugh of Saint Victor, *Exegetica*, I, "Praenotatiunculae in Scripturam sacram," xv (*PL* 175:22–23); and Albert the Great, *Commentarium in Psalmos*, vi, ed. A. Borgnet (Paris, 1891), 14:72.

10. See, e.g., Augustine, *In Joannis Evangelium*, iv.14 (*PL* 35:1465).

11. See, e.g., Martianus Capella, *De nuptiis Philologiae et Mercurii*, vii, ed. F. Eyssenhardt (Leipzig, 1866).

in tetrameter—is significantly that which in each case completes the thought of the stanza.

Each stanza is, in effect, an expanded simple sentence, or, to approach it another way, a statement fragmented into parts that are then restated and echoed, leading to a culmination in the last line. If we approach the stanzas in terms of how they are generated, it is possible to see a series of kernel sentences that are being expanded and enlarged. In stanza 1, the kernel sentence, that which is then fragmented and developed, is "Maiden in the mor lay / Seuenistes fulle ant a day"—the rhyme is not accidental. This relatively simple statement is then echoed in part or in full throughout the stanza. The fragmentation is as follows: "Maiden in the mor lay" exists initially as a complete thought, though a puzzling one; after it is once echoed, an additional element comes into the poem, *seuenyst fulle*, which is likewise echoed; then with line 5, the whole process is repeated, but now the *seuenyst fulle* is continued and perfected with the addition of *ant a day*. The movement has been from what would seem to be a complete utterance through a series of partial ones to a longer phrase that joins to the initial utterance incrementing it. This method may be related to the rhetorical device of merismus (*distributio*) and to the incremental repetition typical of ballad literature. As it works, it allows the audience to focus on different parts of the fragmented thought, to savor each, as it were, and to emphasize certain sounds.

The other stanzas proceed and increment in a way somewhat different from that of stanza 1. Modeled on a question-answer pattern, like the rhetorical figure of anthypophora (*subjectio*), they begin with a statement about the maiden's life on the moor, in the form of "Welle was hire . . . ," which—apparently because it is unusual for *mete, dryng*, and *bour* to be *welle* on a moor—is then questioned. The reply is what is actually fragmented, but still the initial statement-question alternation, as a form of incremental repetition, allows for the kind of echoing that makes these stanzas similar to what was found in the first stanza. The pattern by which the kernel thought is expressed is as follows (based on stanza 2): "Welle was hire mete. Wat? The primerole ant the violet." The query *wat?* breaks what might be appropriately described as a structure of complementation where "the primerole and the violet" redefine or act in apposition to *welle*. In fact, primerole, violet, water, rose, and lily are all to be seen as aspects of *welle;* and in their symbolic significances they show something of the nature of *welle*, that which is the Good. But the wordplay commented on earlier would suggest that *welle* may be both the Good and, as in *welle-spring* (21), the source of all. In both cases it is God, the divine formative and life-giving principle. And *welle* as adjective would then be redefined, as *mor* is redefined in terms of what springs up and occurs on it—the phonic similarity of *mor* in stanza 1 and *bour* and *flour* in stanza 4 would seem to be purposeful.

The other main method of the poem—of all four stanzas in fact—is understatement, as well as a resulting sense of incongruity which comes about because of fragmentation. Through the understatement, there is a building up of expectation as we are led to believe in each stanza that a dramatic conclusion is forthcoming. For instance, after asking over and over what the maiden's food is, the poem leads us to believe that along with *the primerole* will be something else truly significant. There is a dramatic letdown when we find that the something else is *the violet*. Taken as drama and as narrative, the poem is weak and goes nowhere; but if we regard the climax of each stanza as deliberate understatement which demands that we view the work symbolically, we may be able to see its point and power.

The same kind of fragmentation, though to a lesser degree, is found in a related poem linked in manuscript to "Maiden in the mor lay":

> Al nist by the rose, rose—
> Al nist bi the rose i lay;
> Darst ich noust the rose stele,
> Ant yet i bar the flour awey.[12]

Here is the same kind of paradox and restatement that delays the conclusion. The methods and resulting tones of the two poems are so similar that one might well think them to be by the same author or at least of the same popular poetic tradition. This tradition might be described as notable for its use of ballad techniques, indirect statement, and symbolic language to handle a religious subject while still being able to avoid overt didacticism. Also, as is seen in both poems, the tradition makes use of noticeably sensuous language and situations. But like much of the religious verse of the seventeenth-century English metaphysical poets, likewise hinting at sexual double meanings, the lyrics in this tradition may be seen having as their means paradox and ambiguity, and as their ends something that may even be a mystical insight of sorts.

In "Al nist by the rose, rose," we are asked to go beyond the

---

12. Based mainly on Dronke's transcription in "The Rawlinson Lyrics," *N&Q*, 206 (1961), 246; see also Robbins, *Sec*, no. 17, p. 12; and Stevick, *One*, no. 36, p. 59.

sexual situation, presented in terms of the traditional euphemism of plucking a rosebud, so familiar to the later Middle Ages from the *Roman de la Rose*. In one sense this situation may be related to the initial statement of "Maiden in the mor lay," where *lay* and the situation itself are at first ambiguous. But in "Al nist by the rose, rose," where there is a narrator who speaks and an object to which he responds, and where a play between the two is possible, the sexual situation is prolonged to the end. It may be as an afterthought or secondary response that we realize the poem's true subject and theme. Although the narrator did not dare to steal the rose, he still took the flower away with him. If *rose* and *flour* are synonyms, the meaning is that he received that which he could not get himself. Not that the narrator is like Kierkegaard's Knight of Faith, who is given that which he no longer had any hope of getting. Rather, the point has to do with the giving, not with the receiving. Whereas the narrator acts as a manifestation of Platonic *eros*, yearning and desiring love, the rose is an expression of *agape*, complete and all-giving love. This, in Christianity after St. Augustine, is the love of God for man; and here the rose may likely be Mary, who gives herself to God and her son to the world.

This suggestion leads to the other meaning of the paradox, where *rose* may be the larger element and *flour* its essence. Although the narrator did not take the actual rose, he still possessed its quintessence, that which was its meaning and significance. *Flour* had an implication of "virginity,"[13] but such would seem to be here the initial not the final signification of the term. We begin with it as a surface possibility and go from the physical rose to its spiritual part. Having this quintessence, the narrator no longer needs the physical—and this paradox continues to the very end of the poem.

Without understanding the symbolic language in these two poems, we can hardly hope to comprehend their meaning. Only when we view them as being within the Marian and Magdalene traditions do they have any point—this is most true of "Maiden in the mor lay"—and when we see them in this way, we must be astonished at their being collected in a volume of secular verse and being viewed by some critics as utterly nonreligious in nature.[14]

---

13. *OED*, 4:353.

14. Besides Dronke, *N&Q*, pp. 195–96, see Donaldson, pp. 23–24, and Greene, who can only say that "the Maiden herself may have been under a spell or weaving one for sombody else, but we cannot claim for her a religious character or even ecclesiastical approval" (*Speculum*, p. 506). Greene's argument is based on his discovery that a fourteenth-century Irish bishop had composed

Latin songs "to replace worldly songs in the use of cathedral clergy." One of these "worldly" pieces was apparently "Maiden in the mor lay." On the basis of this evidence, Greene concludes that in its own time the lyric was "definitely and explicitly regarded as secular and indeed profane" (p. 504), that it was regarded as something apt to "pollute the throats of the local clergy" (p. 506). But clergy in the late Middle Ages, wanting *doctryne* without *mirthe,* criticized in like manner the vernacular religious drama for its secular nature, even though we today recognize the essential religious symbolism in this drama. See, e.g., the famous Wycliffite treatise against Miracle Plays, in *Reliquiae Antiquae,* ed. T. Wright and J. O. Halliwell (London, 1845), I, 42, summarized in Wells, p. 483. Harris in his forthcoming essay, questions Greene's understanding of the relationship between the Latin poems and the vernacular fragments.

What ys he, thys lordling, that cometh vrom the vyht?
Wyth blod-rede wede so grysliche ydyht,
So vayre ycoyntised, so semlich in syht,
4 So styflyche yongeth, so douhti a knyht.

"Ich hyt am, ich hyt am, that ne speke bote ryht,
Chaunpyoun to helen monkunde in vyht."

Why thoenne ys thy schroud red wyth blod al ymeind,
8 Ase troddares in wrynge wyth most al byspreynd?

"The wrynge ich habbe ytrodded al mysulf on,
And of al monkunde ne was non other won.
Ich hoem habbe ytrodded in wrethe and in grome,
12 And al my wede ys byspreynd wyth hoere blod ysome,
And al my robe yuuled to hoere grete shome.
The day of thylke wreche leueth in my thouht,
The yer of medes-yeldyng ne uoryet ich nouht.
16 Ich loked al aboute som helpynge mon,
Ich souhte al the route, bote help nas ther non.
Hyt was myn oune strengthe that thys bote wrouhte,
Myn owe douhtynesse that help ther me brouhte.
20 On Godes mylsfolnesse ich wole bethenche me,
And heryen hym in alle thyng that he yeldeth me.
Ich habbe ytrodded the uolk in wrethe and in grome,
Adreynt al wyth shennesse, ydrawe doun wyth shome."

Brit. Mus. Addit. MS 46,919 (formerly Phillipps 8336), fol. 210.
Index, no. 3906, p. 625; *Supplement*, p. 446.

Editions:
Brown, *Rel 14*, no. 25, pp. 28–29.
Davies, No. 27, pp. 94095.

Criticism:
Kane, pp. 156–57.
Gneuss, Helmut, "William Hereberts Ubersetzungen," *Anglia*, 78 (1960), 180–86.

A BIBLICAL PARAPHRASE by the early fourteenth-century Franciscan William Herebert, these verses represent a redoing rather than a translation of Isaiah 63:1–7. Technically, the lines may be, as Kane feels, "a poor performance, ill-defined and indeed perhaps also fragmentary," but "the poet's transformation of his material is a real one."[1] Part of the power and interest here is no doubt due to the subject matter which is prophetic, symbolic, and mystical, with many typological connections to the Apocalypse—lines 3 and 7, for instance, may be compared to Apocalypse 19:13—which contains a favorite exegetical symbol of the late Middle Ages, the mystical wine press (8ff.).[2]

But Herebert handles the encounter of the narrator with the Christlike warrior who appears before him—along with the question-answer dialogue—with a directness lacking in the original text. Something of his method may be seen by comparing the first part of the biblical passage with the first lines here. The Vulgate reads, "Quis est iste, qui venit de Edom, tinctis vestibus de Bosra," which may be compared to Herebert's first two lines, "What ys he, thys lordling, that cometh vrom the vyht? / Wyth blod-rede wede so grysliche ydyht." The vague *iste* of the Latin is rendered concretely as *thys lordling*, words not only making the stranger a specific being but suggesting that he is a young man. Moreover, omitting the rather irrelevant detail of his coming from Edom dressed in dyed clothes of Bosra, Herebert states instead that this young warrior has come from *the vyht*, dressed in *blod-rede wede*, and adds that he is *so grysliche ydyht*.

When Herebert returns in lines 3–4 to his original text, it is again to expand it, though in doing so he successfully creates a contrast between the *lordling* who is *vayre* and *semlich* (3) and his *blod-rede wede* (2). Even though we do not exactly know who the lordling is, we know that he is a young warrior who has been in a terrible battle. When he answers the narrator's question (5–6), it is again with a directness totally lacking in the original passage from Isaiah: "Ich hyt am, ich hyt am" (5). This repetition makes us aware of his presence and may even make us feel that we should know the identity of the man. Moreover, "Chaunpyoun to helen monkunde in vyht," with its paradox about healing through fighting, should make us see even more significance in this warrior and in his appearance before us. That Herebert's method is to contract as well as to expand his original may also be seen in the last two couplets of the poem which

---

1. Kane, p. 156.

2. On the mystical wine press, see esp. Emile Mâle, *L'Art religieux de la fin du moyen âge en France*, 4th ed. (Paris, 1931), pp. 115–22.

neatly summarize two biblical verses. Occasionally he follows his original closely—as in the middle lines of his poem—but he also changes the order of his material—as in his last two couplets where he reverses and reinterprets Isaiah 63:6–7, although it has been suggested that his original was flawed and that the change was not his own doing.[3] In any case, it seems clear that Herebert is no slavish translator, that he is using essentials in his material, and that he is interpreting these as he sees fit.

Even more significant, however, is the actual versification the poet uses to create these lines. Doubtless designed for popular consumption as an early instance of the friars' attempt to provide vernacular versions of scripture and liturgy for their parishioners, this piece makes use of something resembling alliteration, a device not frequent in the early fourteenth century—Herebert died in 1333—before the advent of the so-called alliterative revival. But Herebert also plays down this alliteration. First, he does not ordinarily alliterate the stressed syllables—though line 15, with its /ye/ alliteration, and line 23, with its /r/ and /š/ alliteration on alternating stresses, are clearly exceptions; second, he uses rhyme, most often in couplet patterns; and third, he tends to limit and order the number of unstressed syllables, with the result that the ordinary rhythm of the lines may be diagrammed as amphibrachic tetrameter: $X/X|X/X||X/X|X/(X)$. Each line most often contains a series of four stresses, sometimes with a caesura dividing the line into half-lines, and sometimes with the final foot being iambic and thereby masculine.

Furthermore, while the key words in each line commonly receive the stress, these words are often paralleled by related key words in other lines. In lines 7–8, for example—"Why thoenne ys thy schroud red wyth blod al ymeind, / Ase troddares in wrynge wyth most al byspreynd?"—the third-stressed *blod* and *most* (grape juice) are clearly related, as are the fourth-stressed *ymeind* (drenched) and *byspreynd* (sprinkled). But the real related elements are the phrases that contain these key words: "wyth blod al ymeind" (7) is echoed by "wyth most al byspreynd" (8). Such a parallel brings into the poem the image of the wine press—frequently symbolizing the wrath of God[4]—in terms of the fight and sacrifice of the young warrior and

---

3. See, e.g., Brown, *Rel 14*, p. 254n.

4. This signification, frequently relating to Apocalypse 14:18–20, where the vintage of the earth is described as being thrown "into the great wine press of the wrath of God" ("in lacum irae Dei magnum"), was common in the Middle Ages. See, e.g., *Die Apokalypse*, ed. Paul Kristeller (Berlin, 1916), pl. 29; and

leads to the dominant imagery of the explanation that follows. The first line of the question (7) contains a statement of what in fact is— the clothing is red with blood—and the next line creates the simile about the wine press to give certain connotations to this fact.

Sometimes, however, Herebert's principle is to develop by means of an incremental repetition of sorts. This method may be seen clearly in lines 12–13–"And al my wede ys byspreynd wyth hoere blod ysome, / And al my robe yuuled to hoere grete shome"–where, by paralleling and repeating phrases, he moves from the general to the particular. The condition of the *wede* is essentially repeated in the condition of the *robe*, with the main differences that the more general *wede* is particularized in the *robe*, and that besprinkling (*byspreynd*), now described as a befouling (*yuuled*), is both particularized and given a distinctly pejorative association. It is this association that leads to the second half-line, "to hoere grete shome" (13), which replaces the more innocent "wyth hoere blod ysome" (12). The converse may be found in the next couplet: "The day of thylke wreche leueth in my thouht, / The yer of medes-yeldyng ne uoryet ich nouht" (14–15). In the first stress the lesser and more specific *day* (14) is expanded to the greater and more general *yer* (15). The principle of incremental repetition is, moreover, expressed in terms of good and bad, positive and negative, functioning to give an examination, as it were, of all sides of the issue: *wreche* (vengeance, 14) leads to *medes-yeldyng* (reward-giving, 15), a reexpression of a negative in terms of a positive. The last parts of the two lines are in a similar contrast, with "leueth in my thouht" changing to "ne uoryet ich nouht"–though now the positive is reexpressed as a negative.

In the next two couplets (16–17, 18–19) incremental repetition is similarly the dominant structural principle. In lines 16–17, the development is first from the general to the particular, from *loked* to *souhte;* then the reverse, from *helpynge mon* to *help*, with the additional change from a positive to a negative expression. In lines 18–19, the repetition is more of a restatement using synonyms for the key words: from *strengthe* to the equivalent *douhtynesse*, from *bote* (remedy) to the equivalent *help*. It might be noted that both *bote* and *help* had been placed together in line 17, "*bote help* nas ther non," though there *bote*, of course, meant "but." Still these two *botes* are phonetically close enough to bring into the poem a sense of

---

André Lejard, *Les tapisseries de l'Apocalypse de la Cathédrale d'Angers* (Paris, 1942), pl. 57.

paronomasia; and, although it may be pushing the wordplay too far, the two morphemes may even be seen suggested in the line before this one—"a*boute* som *help*ynge mon" (16). After appearing joined together, the terms are then separated in successive lines, *bote* changing its meaning and *help* moving from a positive to a negative.

Two further instances of repetition may profitably be examined. First, certain key terms are repeated several times throughout the poem: the morpheme *trod*, for instance, appears in lines 8, 9, 11, and 22, always as a stressed base. In like manner, there are repetitions or near-repetitions of phrases, clauses, and, in one instance, a whole line—11 is repeated in 22, the lines differing only in that the pronoun *hoem* (11) is restated in the form of determiner and noun, *the uolk* (22). Such repetitions serve to hold together the poem, allowing its thoughts and images to be both emphasized and kept in mind. The last instance of repetition to be examined is that described rhetorically as anaphora (*repetitio*). Whereas it appears sporadically throughout the poem, it may be seen in the initial four lines, all linked through their rhyme and through their forming the opening question of the poem. In lines 2–4, the word *so* is repeated five times, in each case introducing a phrase that, as a structure of modification, refers back to the *lordling* (1). But as the phrases expand our understanding of this being, so they present us with his paradoxical nature: he is both terribly arrayed (*grysliche ydyht*) and fair appareled or pleasant in appearance (*vayre ycoyntised*). Being joined by the same *so*, these opposite descriptions have the appearance of equivalents joined in a coordinate construction, with *so* both functioning as an adverb of intensity and at the same time seeming to contain a sense of the conjunction "and." Line 4 continues these *so* phrases but presents an additional problem. *So styflyche yongeth* seems at first to be a continuation of the adverbial construction plus verbal (as past participle) seen in the first two phrases, but *yongeth* gets in the way.

In his hesitating translation of the phrase as "(who) goes so sturdily (?)," Davies recognizes the problem.[5] Were the phrase to mean this, it would, with its new verb and syntax, be a flaw in the coordinate nature of the construction: it would wrongly take our attention away from the *lordling* who is coming (*cometh*, 1), not going; and it would not lead easily to the phrase in the second half of line 4, "so douhti a knyht." On the other hand, were the word to mean "youth"— that is, were we to read the phrase as though it were "so sturdy a youth"—the problem of reference and of context would be eliminated.

---

5. Davies, p. 94.

It is not even necessary to claim that *yongeth* is the result of a sloppy minim, resulting in *n* instead of *u*; for, according to the *OED, youngeth* is a possible variant for "youth."[6] At the same time, we might well think of *styflyche* as *styflych a*. Reading the line in this way, we may see the first half, "so sturdy a youth," parallels the second half, "so doughty a knight." Both substantives *yongeth* and *knyht* would furthermore refer back to *lordling*, providing emphasis on his youth and nobility. With the accompanying change of *styflyche* to *styflych a*, the grammatical problem of *styflyche* as an adverb would also be removed, though it should be recognized that *styf* rather than *styflych* is the common Middle English adjectival form. It may not be too much to claim, however, that, whatever the particular meaning of the phrase, the suggestion of "youth" is contained in the word *yongeth*, and this is the element that is then developed in the next half-line into *knyht*.

The descriptive terms *styflych(e)* and *douhti* also contrast with the *semlich* of the previous line and serve to continue the paradox of the *lordling's* appearance and nature already suggested by the juxtaposition of *grysliche* (2) and *vayre* (3). The paradox is essentially that seen by the Christian Middle Ages as contained in and stemming from the color red. Symbolizing the ecclesiastical virtue of charity, it was associated with Christ, typically as the color of his halo. But at the same time, it was associated with evil, with wrath, and with the hell fire that will punish sinful man.[7] This color is also related to the wine press as a destructive machine representing God's wrath. With Christ, however, this press and the color red are to be associated with redemption through sacrifice and love.[8] The fighting and killing done

---

6. *OED*, 12:74. Even though the manuscript is a holograph, there are instances of sloppy writing on Herebert's part, as indicated by emendations in Brown and in Gneuss, esp. pp. 180–86.

7. On this as the *significatio in malo* of red, see, e.g., René Gilles, *Le symbolisme dans l'art religieux*, 2d ed. (Paris, 1943), p. 106.

8. See esp. Maurice Vloberg, *L'Eucharistie dans l'art* (Grenoble, 1946), 2: 172–83; and several illustrations, esp. that in the *Hortus deliciarum* of Herrade of Landsberg. For the theological basis of the concept, see, e.g., Augustine, *Ennarationes in Psalmos*, LV (*PL* 36:649); and Peter Damian, *Sermo*, L (*PL* 144:786). See also Mâle, p. 116, and figs. 63–65. For other artistic representations in the late Middle Ages showing Christ, generally on the Cross, treading the wine press, see A. W. Byvanck, *La miniature dans les Pays-Bas septentrionaux*, trans. A. Haye (Paris, 1937), pl. 9, fig. 16; André Blum, *Les origines de la gravure en France* (Paris, 1927), pl. 26, fig. 31; and Erwin Panofsky, *Albrecht Dürer* (Princeton, 1943), 2: 9, 73. In one interesting woodcut, the blood of Christ pours out as wine from his wounds while the cross acts as a wine press being operated by God the father (*Fifteenth Century Woodcuts and Metalcuts from the National Gallery of Art*, Washington, D.C., n.d., pl. 124). The note to this

by Christ as *chaunpyoun* is that which ideally will *helen monkunde* (6), even though it has resulted in Christ's death. Through *wreth, grome,* and *shome* (22–23), repeated from earlier in the poem, man killed Christ; but also through Christ's sacrifice man may learn of God's *mylsfolnesse* (20). Emphasized here are the sacrifice and the *shennesse* (humiliation) and *shome* (23), not the reward. Man may realize what, because of Christ's sacrifice, is now in store for him; but he must know his own responsibility and guilt as one who has caused the death of his *chaunpyoun.*

---

plate, citing Isaiah 63:34, states that "this allegorical image summons up a vengeful Christ for the Day of Judgment and lashes out at the lack of understanding of the crucifixion." On the cross as wine press, see also the Middle English "Dispute between Mary and the Cross," l. 2 (in *Legends of the Holy Rood,* ed. Richard Morris, EETS OS 41, London, 1871, p. 138).

I sayh hym with fless al bisprad—
    He cam vram est;
I sayh hym with blod al byssad—
4   He cam vram west.
I sayh thet manye he with hym broughte—
    He cam vram south;
I sayh thet the world of hym ne roughte—
8   He cam vram north.

I come vram the wedlok as a svete spouse,
    thet habbe my wif with me innome.
I come vram vight a staleworthe knyght,
12   thet myne vo habbe ouercome.
I come vram the chepyng as a riche chapman,
    thet mankynde habbe ibought.
I come vram an uncouthe londe as a sely pylegrym,
16   thet ferr habbe isought.

Merton Coll. Oxford, MS. 248, fol. 139v.
Index, no. 1353, p. 214; no. 1289, p. 204; *Supplement,* pp. 161, 152.

Editions:
    Brown, *Rel 14,* no. 36, pp. 52–53.

Criticism:
    Kane, p. 157.
    Manning, *Wisdom,* pp. 19–21.

THIS UNUSUAL POEM, which has been markedly neglected,[1] is within the apocalyptic and visionary traditions so important in medieval writing. But its existence as a poem has even been denied by some;[2] and according to the Brown and Robbins *Index* and its *Supplement,* the stanzas represent two different works. In manuscript these lines follow a Latin sermon containing the same themes found in them, and the second stanza is an actual translation of a passage from the preceding page.[3] Moreover, even though the attempt at rhyme shows a clear intention to create verse, and even though the pervasive ana-phora (*repetitio*) may indicate a conscious artistry, the lines are metrically awkward, so much so that at times they read like prose. Still, as will be shown, the two stanzas work together to produce a unified whole that is a compelling, even powerful piece of literature.

Although both Brown and Manning view the work as being in the form of eight long lines—with the shorter lines of the first stanza separated from the longer ones by a caesura—such a division seems awkward and misleading. Whereas the last stanza is doubtless a four-sentence unit—being what Manning terms monostrophic[4]—the rhymes of the first stanza show that it is really in the form of two quatrains. In the second stanza, where each sentence is divided into parallel parts, there may be a similarity to the organization typical of hymns, where in some cases the traditionally long heptameter lines may be broken into tetrameters and trimeters. But for ease of citation, if nothing else, the piece is here presented as though it were composed of sixteen lines.

The lyric begins from the point of view of the narrator who de-scribes a vision he had of the coming of Christ—the long lines showing the appearance of Christ, the shorter, even-numbered ones describing in the directional variations his omnipresence. Coming from all four points of the compass, Christ occupies the center and pervades every-thing, his Second Coming suggesting, it would seem, that Judgment Day is at hand; appropriately, the second stanza then shows Christ speaking. But in stanza 1, the foreground is occupied by the narrator and his description of the vision at hand. This stanza—in the form of two quatrains—is divided in the middle. Even though *I sayh* begins each long line in this stanza, lines 1 and 3, followed by *hym with,*

---

1. The analysis in Manning, however, is especially good.

2. E.g., Kane, who, after saying that the piece is "highly imaginative," concludes that it is "ill-formed to the extent of hardly being a poem at all" (p. 157).

3. The Latin is quoted in Brown, *Rel 14,* p. 258n.

4. Manning, *Wisdom,* p. 21.

make up simple sentences; whereas in lines 5 and 7, where the *I sayh* is followed by a *thet* clause, the sentences are complex.

Lines 1 and 3 are also unified through their descriptions of the person of Christ. He is first "with fless al bisprad," literally covered or overspread with flesh; but the line is ambiguous in that the description may suggest both Christ's appearing in the form of man and his being spread out on the cross. Although both meanings may be supported by line 3, where Christ is shown "with blod al byssad," drenched with blood, the dominant connotation seems to be his death and, further, his sacrifice. Ironically, however, at the same time that Christ is described as dying or dead, he is shown to be very much alive—his coming from all directions makes us aware of his presence. At first, the short lines may seem puzzling inasmuch as, in the context of lines 1 and 3, we might expect them to describe Christ on the cross; but if we realize that the four points of the cross, like those of a medieval church, were seen reflecting the four directions of the compass, we may understand the unity of thought here. More significantly, the Day of Judgment is presented as stemming from the crucifixion; and Christ, first seen as victim helpless on the cross (1, 3), is now shown coming back to man triumphantly as all-powerful judge.

The fifth and seventh lines present the world's response to Christ. Line 5, showing him bringing *manye* with him, may suggest the heavenly host accompanying him; but it mainly refers to mankind, which has been saved by Christ's shedding his blood, thus continuing the thought of line 3. This view is reinforced by line 7, in which *the world* occupies the same place in the syntax as *manye* did; and both terms apparently have a relationship similar to that found in *fless* and *blod* (1, 3). But line 7 is also opposed to Christ's totally successful salvation of mankind. Even on this special day, it would seem, "the world of hym ne roughte." In this sense *the world* would represent those who were not saved and would function connotatively as the opposite of the *manye*. Similarly, *ne roughte*, "did not care," counters *broughte* (5), those who cared and who came to and with Christ.

There may also be a conscious pattern to the short even-numbered lines—which also exist in rhyming or near-rhyming pairs—that ties in with the meanings of the longer odd-numbered lines. The east (2) seems to be associated through the rising sun with Christ's Incarnation, suggested in the previous line's ambiguous reference to his birth; the west (4), with the setting sun, is the place of death, and

appropriately follows the line about bloodshed suggesting the crucifixion. Similarly, the south (6), symbolizing the True Church (*Ec-
clesia*), is linked to the line about Christ's redeeming man; and the
north (8), traditional place of hell and symbol of False Belief (*Syna-
goga*), is appropriate to those who are uncaring and who have re-
jected Christ.[5]

The relationship of the two stanzas is such that the second both
derives from the first and presents the same situation from a different
point of view. In stanza 2, Christ is talking, revealing his own nature
and the purpose of his coming; and the tense shifts from past *sayh*
to present *come*, which picks up the *cam* of the even-numbered lines
in stanza 1. What was being reported is now at hand. The structure is
such that what is here presented as two lines provides a complete
syntactic unit, with what begins in the first line being completed in
the second by means of an adjectival clause referring back to the last
word of the previous line. The references themselves are to different
aspects of the human situation and to different professions. First,
Christ is like *a svete spouse* (9) who has taken his wife. The word for
"taken," *innome* (10), is ambiguous and would seem to mean other
than that Christ is like a husband who has taken his wife with him
from their wedding. The construction, "thet habbe my wif with me
innome," has distinct sexual connotations and suggests the consumma-
tion of the marriage. Such an image may seem grotesque here in reference to Christ, but it is only an extension of what appeared in line
1 of the poem, where Christ is described as being "with fless al bisprad." What seemed there to be possibly a description of death now
appears in this first sentence of stanza 2 as the creation of life; but the
emphasis is mainly on the state of *wedlok* that is to be seen as a victory

---

5. See Manning (ibid., pp. 20, 33n.), who refers to Gregory the Great,
Homiliae in Ezechielem, 1 (*PL* 76:940); also Emile Mâle, *The Gothic Image,*
trans. Dora Hussey (New York, 1958), pp. 5–6; and Louis Réau, *Iconographie
de l'art chrétien* (Paris, 1955), 1:70–71. The image seems to be related to the motif, common in iconography, showing the blood from the feet of the crucified
Christ flowing onto a globe beneath, representing the earth. See, e.g., *The Hours
of Catherine of Cleves,* intro. and comm. John Plummer (New York, n.d.), pls. 38,
39; and Max J. Friedlaender, *Early Netherlandish Painting from Van Eyck to
Bruegel,* trans. M. Kay (London, 1965), pl. 171. In the Middle English *Mirk's
Festial,* the east is referred to as the place of Christ's church, of paradise, of
calvary, and of the Second Coming. In this respect Mirk writes, "Also thenke
that Cryst schall com out of the est to the dome, wherfor ye schull pray to hym
to yeue you such contrisyon of hert for your mys-dedys, and apon scheryft wyth
mowthe and satysfaccyon yn dede that ye may be sure forto stond on Cristys
ryght hond yn that dome" (ed. Theodor Erbe, EETS ES 96, London, 1905, 1:
279).

over the *fless*—though Manning also points out, on the basis of such passages as Psalms 18:6, that *wedlok* is an expression of Christ's Incarnation.[6]

In like manner, the other three sentences of this stanza refer to and redefine the other long lines of stanza 1. Lines 11–12, describing Christ as coming "vram vight a staleworthe knyght," who has overcome his foe, refer to his being "with blod al byssad" (3). Again, what was seen as death appears as life; and, moreover, the earlier suggestion of defeat is here transformed into victory. The reference to *myne vo* (12) would seem to point to the devil whom Christ, through his sacrifice on the cross, has defeated for man. Similarly, the earlier description of Christ's bringing *manye* with him (5) is presented in this second stanza in terms of the business dealings of a merchant, a *riche chapman* (13), suggesting further the nature and success of Christ's saving mankind, of his being the redeemer of all.

But it is the final sentence that is the most surprising. Describing Christ as a *sely* (poor) pilgrim from an unknown land who *ferr habbe isought* (15–16), it refers to his being alone and scorned, the image found in line 7 of the earlier stanza, showing the world's not caring about him. Here, however, appears more than pathos; for the state of the *sely pylegrym* is the proper condition of man, who should be seeking his final dwelling place and who should view his life in this world as a pilgrimage away from the world. It is the culminating image in a group presenting Christ's struggle, which is also symbolically man's, to overcome world (7, 15–16), flesh (1, 9–10), devil (3, 11–12), and death (5, 13–14). But this popular commonplace is not treated in the poem in a way that is openly didactic or even typical, and it would clearly be wrong to reduce the lyric to the terms of this concept or even to say that it is openly celebrating the ecclesiastical virtues of faith, hope, and charity. The concept would seem rather to provide the reference points for the imagery, but the usual progression—world, flesh, devil—is not adhered to or emphasized.

What is emphasized, on the other hand, is Christ's being "a sely pylegrym / thet ferr habbe isought" (15–16). This description continues the identities of previous lines where Christ is *a svete spouse, a staleworthe knyght,* and *a riche chapman*—the adjectives in each case being appropriate for creating a nonpareil. But the last identity, where the adjective *sely* also is the appropriate one, shows that the redemption is unfinished. Throughout this stanza the auxiliary *habbe*

---

6. Manning, *Wisdom*, p. 20. This idea is, of course, related to the Christian allegorical interpretation of the Song of Solomon, where Christ is seen as a bridegroom.

(has) acts to complete the action being presented: the spouse *has*, already as it were, taken his wife; similarly, the knight *has* overcome his foe, and the chapman *has* bought mankind. But in the final sentence the *habbe* does not refer to any completed act. Here the pilgrim has sought far; whether he has found what he was seeking or not, the end of his journey does not seem to be at hand. Man has not been saved and the attempt to save him is not over. Rather than celebrate victory, the poem at the conclusion gives the impression of Christ's continuing love for man—even though "the world of hym ne roughte" (7). For all its apocalyptic suggestions, this poem is finally not about Doomsday at all, with an all-powerful stern God judging mankind, but about a gentle sympathetic Christ's concern to save man. The final image of Christ as a poor pilgrim is a deliberate alteration of what we are led to expect, and with its reversal of roles it provides an intentional anticlimax. Whereas man should be the pilgrim and seek Christ, here Christ is the pilgrim, "vran an vncouthe londe," searching for man.[7] To be a pilgrim is also to renounce such joys and concerns of the world as are represented earlier in the second stanza by wedlock, military combat, and business transactions. It is primarily to do penance, to humble oneself, and to ask forgiveness for one's sins. Christ is thus shown continuing to take man's sins on his shoulders.

In manuscript these two stanzas are followed by two more which are entirely unnecessary and clearly not to be considered as part of this poem. Based on Apocalypse 5:2–5, they show Christ in the guise of each of the Four Horsemen of the Apocalypse, who in all cases are seen as serving rather than as destroying man.[8] Whereas these stanzas are interesting in their own right, they are related to the sixteen lines presented here only by virtue of their being apocalyptic.

---

7. The tradition of Christ as a pilgrim seems to have been peculiar to the late Middle Ages, perhaps being derived from the three *Pèlerinages* of Guillaume Deguileville in the early fourteenth century, especially the *Pèlerinage de Jésus-Christ*. Jesus, before his incarnation, is sent forth as a little child by the Father, with the staff and scrip of a pilgrim; quoted in Adolphe N. Didron, *Christian Iconography*, trans. M. Stokes (London, 1886), 1:294ff; see also the discussion that follows and the fourteenth-century illustrations in figs. 75, 78. Cf. Mrs. Jameson, *The History of Our Lord* (London, 1865), 2:377–78; A. W. Byvanck, *La miniature dans les Pays-Bas septentrionaux*, trans. A. Haye (Paris, 1937), pl. 11, fig. 25; and the Wolgemut woodcut of Christ as pilgrim in Richard Bellin, "Wolgemuts Skizzenbuch," in *Studien zur Deutschen Kunstgeschichte*, 332 (Baden Baden, 1959), pl. 1, fig. 4 rect. Also in Duccio's painting of Christ's appearing to the apostles on the road to Emmaus (Luc 24:13ff.), Christ is shown as a pilgrim with staff and wallet with scallop shells; see, e.g., Emilio Cecchi, *The Sienese Painters of the Trecento*, trans. L. Penlock (London, 1931), pl. 51.

8. See Brown, *Rel 14*, p. 258n.

Still, even this apocalyptic quality is here softened or reduced; for this poem, ending with Christ in the role of pilgrim, presents a definite and deliberate understatement: the imminent hellfire and damnation give way to continual forgiveness. Finally, the lyric may or may not be a totally finished product, but containing what it does and stopping where it does, it is complete and effective.

Vndo thi dore, my spuse dere,
Allas! wy stond i loken out here?
    Fre am i thi make.
4 Loke mi lokkes and ek myn heued
And al my bodi with blod beweued,
    For thi sake.

Allas, allas! heuel haue i sped:
8 For senne Iesu is fro me fled,
    Mi trewe fere.
Withouten my gate he stant alone,
Sorfuliche he maket his mone
12   On his manere.

Lord, for senne i sike sore,
Foryef, and i ne wil no more;
With al my mith senne i forsake,
16 And opne myn herte the inne to take.
For thin herte is clouen oure loue to kecchen,
Thi loue is chosen vs alle to fecchen;
Min herte it therlede, yef i wer kende,
20 Thi suete loue to hauen in mende.
Perce myn herte with thi louengge,
That in the i haue my duellingge.
    Amen.

Advocates Lib. MS 18.7.21, fol. 121v.
Index, no. 3825, p. 613; *Supplement*, p. 435.

Editions:
Brown, *Rel 14*, no. 68, p. 86.

Criticism:
Manning, *Wisdom*, pp. 125–26.

WITHIN THE TRADITION that centers on the dichotomy between the all-giving love of Christ and the hardheartedness or unconcern of man, this poem combines two forms. First, it is a dialogue between Christ and man at the moment when man realizes that in his sinfulness he is apart from Christ; and, second, it is a personal prayer for forgiveness and an assurance by the narrator that he will hitherto be receptive to Christ. But it is also a studied ambiguity artfully contrived, which deserves to be better known.[1] The text seems to be taken from the well-known episode in Canticles 5:2–6, where the bridegroom, identified in medieval exegesis as Christ, knocks at the door, and the speaker voices her response to him but does not open the door in time for him to enter. The text may also be related to Apocalypse 3:20: "Ecce sto ad ostium; et pulso."[2]

The dominant image of the piece is love: man is called Christ's *spuse dere* (1), and promises to receive the love of Christ, whose heart was *clouen* (17) to save man and obtain his love. Related to this theme, though not vividly or explicitly presented, is an ambiguous kind of sexual imagery that describes both the piercing of man's heart by Christ (21) and the parallel piercing of Christ's heart—through the stab from Longinus' spear—so that he can receive man's love (17). But if such a suggestion is valid, the sexual imagery is subdued and, while perhaps distinctly related to a mystical kind of union, is hardly a major motif in the poem. The explicit image presents man's heart as a dwelling that has shut out Christ, who is the *make* (3) or *fere* (9) of the house's owner—though at the end Christ becomes the house or macrocosm, since in him is necessarily man's true *duellingge* (22).

The dialogue begins with Christ's appearing as a stranger or outcast, addressing man who is withdrawn within his own world, that of his hard heart. Christ's words about his being allowed to enter are in the form of a request not a command, and he resembles a returned wanderer who deserves more of a reception that he has received. It is an injustice for him not to be greeted enthusiastically and received warmly. His claim is, first, that he is man's *make* (3) and, second, that he has sacrificed himself for man's sake (4–6). At this point in the

---

1. It is collected only in Brown, *Rel 14*; Manning's analysis, though brief, is revealing.

2. As it exists in Brown and in the Brown and Robbins *Index*, the poem has as its title the line from Apocalypse. For exegesis of this passage, see, e.g., Alexander of Hales, *Expositio in Apocalypsim*, ed. A. Wachtel, MGH, Quellen zur Geistesgeschichte des Mittelalters (Weimar, 1955), 1:48, and Richard Rolle of Hampole, *Tractatus super Apocalypsim*, ed. and trans. N. Marzac (Paris, 1968), pp. 154–56.

poem, however, it is not clear that the stranger is Christ; and our initial response is to the dramatic suggestiveness of the stanza rather than to any message contained within it. Also, it is nowhere explicit that Christ is here addressing mankind in general, although the narrator, who later identifies the outsider as *Iesu* (8), comes to stand for unthinking, ungrateful, sinful man. The second stanza presents the narrator's response to the entreaty from without, and, as his initial utterance *allas, allas!* (7) shows, he is immediately full of contrition for the sinfulness that has kept the thought of Christ from him: "For senne Iesu is fro me fled" (8). Following this is his real concern for Christ who *stant alone* (10) when he could be welcomed by the narrator. The next stanza proceeds directly to his prayer for forgiveness, and the poem ends without a return to the dramatic situation with which it began.

The dialogue in the first two stanzas is something other than a debate or even a confrontation. Taking place at the moment when man realizes what he has done, it presents an externalization of the narrator's conscience, which is then acknowledged by the narrator. This poem is consequently different from the many poems that present Christ's appeal to man or his statement of man's inherent forgetfulness and hypocrisy. In relation to these poems this lyric begins where they leave off and shows the narrator's acknowledgment of guilt and his intention to rectify matters; it also lacks the heavy-handed pathos and overstatement that mark some related works. The fictional situation allows prayer to be mingled with, and put in a context of, drama; and, furthermore, the didacticism inherent in this and such works is here couched in lines that are very much concerned with the interplay of sounds and words.

The first two stanzas are each in the form of two triads, with two tetrameters culminating in a dimeter (though line 3 is a trimeter), rhyming *aabccb*. It is a verse form frequently found in Middle English lyrics, and one especially suitable for stopping a thought without giving the impression that it is exhausted. The short concluding line often contains a significant or repeated phrase that, in standing out, is able to assume an importance it might not have had in a longer line. Also this stanzaic pattern allows for a certain amount of repetition and reiteration, and the second triad in each of the first two stanzas acts as a restatement, in a sense, of the first triad. For instance, the first three lines show Christ expressing his inability to understand why he has been kept outside; and the second triad continues this thought but has Christ present the reasons for his deserving to enter

—in a statement of his having died for man that makes us further aware of the injustice of the situation.

Whereas the first triad, beginning *in mediis rebus*, confronts us with a particular strange situation, the second triad helps identify the speaker and focuses our attention on his person. The first lines begin with a request—the direct address to *my spuse dere* softening the command of *vndo thi dore;* but the second group of three lines shows no such tempering of an imperative. With the command *loke* (4), narrator and audience alike are called on to regard the person of the speaker and see how his *lokkes, heued,* and *bodi* are all enveloped (*beweued*) with blood (5). It is the final short line of the stanza, however, that drives home the injustice: all the suffering is *for thi sake* (6), as again the audience is brought into the poem and made to feel the guilt. In the earlier triad, the emphasis on *my spuse dere* and on the speaker's being *thi make* has made everything seem gentle and kind; but if the relationship between man and Christ is as unconscious and precarious as is presented here, man's guilt is all the more; and *for thi sake* underscores this. In another sense the marriage imagery of this stanza makes Christ's exile from man seem all the more heinous and the narrator's attitude all the more vicious. But the use of *fre* in line 3 is somewhat strange. One relevant meaning of *fre* in line 3 is somewhat strange. One relevant meaning of *fre* in Middle English is "possessing the rights and privileges of a citizen,"[3] and in saying, "Fre am i thi make," the speaker may be claiming his right to enter and be within. Because of the syntax the line may then be read, "Deserving am I, your mate," with *thi make* thus being in apposition with *i* and a basis, as it were, for Christ's claims on the narrator's heart.[4]

In stanza 2 the narrator's ejaculatory *allas, allas!* (7) both shows his recognition of what he has done and refers to the earlier *allas,* spoken by Christ in line 2; but the grief is here all the more since the identity of the speaker and the enormity of man's sin have become clear. With Christ asking to be admitted, it may seem incongruous for the narrator to claim that Jesus has fled from him (8); but the sense is really that the narrator has, perhaps unintentionally but

---

3. *MED*, 3:871 (*fre*, 3.b.).

4. Another possibility is that *fre* is really to be read as *vre* (Fr. *vrai*), the pronunciation of the grapheme *f* as a voiced fricative being common in Middle English. As such, the word may act as a conjunctive adverb meaning "truly" or "really," but the inversion of the next words *am i* makes this possibility somewhat remote. In either case, the line emphasizes Christ's claim on the narrator.

nevertheless actually, shut out Christ. Contrition has led to his con-
fession of guilt, and, ideally, satisfaction will follow. As the poem is
organized, however, it is not initially clear that the narrator's complaint is what is being presented in the last section. At the end of
stanza 2, when Christ is described as standing alone—"Sorfuliche he
maket his mone / On his mannere" (11–12)—it is Christ's *mone* that
we expect to hear. A similar discrepancy between the expected and
the actual occurs with stanza 2. As the *allas* there picks up the earlier
one, uttered by Christ, we may justifiably think that we are continuing to hear Christ speaking; at least this is a valid impression
until the second line of the stanza.

The full acknowledgment of sin, as well as a verbal kind of satisfaction, is the substance of stanza 3. The narrator grieves (*sike sore*,
13) for his sin—the phrase *for senne* is picked up from line 8 and
echoed here; if he is forgiven, he will sin no longer (14); he promises
to forsake sin with all his strength (*mith*, 15) and to open his heart to
Christ (16). The two couplets containing these thoughts are related
and make a unit somewhat different from what is found in the rest of
the stanza. In what follows the narrator stops talking about how he
will change and looks to Christ's love, which is described in complex language:

> For thin herte is clouen oure loue to kecchen,
> Thi loue is chosen vs alle to fecchen;
> Min herte it therlede, yef i wer kende,
> Thi suete loue to hauen in mende. (17–20)

The meaning of the first two lines here would seem to be that Christ's
heart has been opened (*clouen*) to receive our love—perhaps also
that Christ has died for man—and this love has resolved (*chosen*)
to rescue all mankind. The terms *thin herte* (17) and *thi loue* (18)
appear as near synonyms, and these are indeed the key words in this
last part of the poem.

The next two lines (19–20) are even more confusing. The sense of
line 19 seems to be that Christ's love (*it*) would pierce (*therlede*)
the narrator's heart if he were well-disposed (*kende*) to receiving it.
But *kende*, a variant of *kinde*, also seems to mean "natural," as opposed to "perverse or depraved." It is unnatural for the narrator to
close his heart to Christ, just as it would be unnatural for him to lock
out his spouse (1). But the connection between lines 19 and 20 is not
easily seen. "Thi suete loue to hauen in mende" (20) may seem to
relate to "yef i wer kende" (19) in the sense of being a parallel to it.
That is, the construction may be, "If I were kind and if I had your

sweet love in mind, it would pierce my heart." Or, the statement in line 20 may be the result of the piercing, which has in turn resulted from the narrator's receptivity, his being *kende*, in the sense that to be *kende* is to allow one's heart to be pierced, which is here to permit Christ's *suete loue* to enter. In this sense *mende* (20) would be seen as synonymous with *herte* (19). The splitting of Christ's *herte* (17) is thus echoed in the piercing of man's heart, and man's love will become, as it were, like Christ's love.

The interplay of forces continues further in the last couplet of the poem: "Perce myn herte with thi louengge, / That in the i haue my duellingge" (21–22). Here the theoretical possibility becomes an actual, wished for, and requested thing. The narrator's imperative *perce myn herte* may be seen also as a response to Christ's imperative *vndo thi dore* in the first line. Not only has the narrator consented to this request, he seems to be demanding in return that love enter him. The imagery of life and death continues with an ambiguity that mirrors the surface confusion in lines 17–20, where Christ's love and man's love are related, and where the hearts of both Christ and man are pierced. It is clear enough in lines 21–22 as to who is doing what to whom, but it would seem that the narrator's being pierced with Christ's love would make the narrator filled with Christ—or, to say it another way, that Christ would live in him. In the last line, however, this expected conclusion is reversed: Christ's piercing the narrator will result in the narrator's dwelling in Christ (*the*, 22). The meaning is, of course, that Christ's love will save man and allow his soul to enter the Empyrean and have its dwelling there with Christ. The *duellingge* of line 22 is very different from that whose *dore* is mentioned in line 1, and by giving up his own self, by breaking the shell that keeps our Love, man is able to change his very being. At the same time, Christ and Love are to be seen as synonyms whose opposite is *senne*, specifically here a kind of self-love or self-containment through which man shuts out the all-giving, all-creating love of God.

Throughout the entire poem the sounds seem to be chosen with care and with an ear to interplaying patterns and subpatterns. Alliteration is noticeable in almost every line except the short ones, sometimes being in the form of one dominant sound, as in line 1 with its three *d* phonemes, or as two or more sounds, as in line 2 with its alternating *l*'s and *o*'s. The sounds also lead to the play of homonyms in line 4, with *loke* and *lokkes*, words that also look back to and pick up *loken* in line 2. Line 4 is also a good example of what may be effected through the consistently careful balancing of sounds: "Loke mi lokkes and ek myn heued." Not only do the *l*'s and *o*'s alliterate, so do the *k*'s, as reinforced by *ek*, whose vowel sound may be related to that in *heued*—at least they are in the same relationship as the *o*'s of the line. Moreover, even the unstressed *mi* and *myn* are phonologically related, reinforcing a tendency throughout the lyric toward an interplay of the words for "my," "thy," and "I," helping to create the ambiguity that is built up so effectively as the poem develops. It is this ambiguity, specifically the blend of roles, that ultimately makes the poem the interesting composition it is.

Gold and al this werdis wyn
Is nouth but Cristis rode;
I wolde ben clad in Cristes skyn,
4 That ran so longe on blode,
And gon t'is herte and taken myn in—
Ther is a fulsum fode.
Than yef i litel of kith or kyn,
8 For ther is alle gode.
Amen.

Advocates Lib. MS 18.7.21, fol. 124v, col. 2.
Index, no. 1002, p. 160; *Supplement*, p. 117.

Editions:
Brown, *Rel 14*, no. 71, p. 88.
Davies, no. 49, p. 130.

Criticism:
Kane, p. 139.
Dronke, *ML*, p. 70.
Reiss, *Style*, pp. 102–06.

ALTHOUGH THE GROTESQUERIE of this piece may startle a modern reader, such language is traditional in the religious writing of the Middle Ages, in both vernacular poems and Latin hymns. Not only did medieval man wish to "ben clad in Cristes skyn" (3), he also imagined hiding himself in the wound in Christ's side.[1] Such desires would seem to be based on the wish to identify with Christ, masochistically perhaps to suffer with him, as in this poem when the narrator dwells on the detail that the skin "ran so longe on blode" (4). But the identification with Christ also enabled man to participate in his perfection and to achieve the salvation brought by him. This is certainly the point of line 5, which states man's desire to make his dwelling in Christ's heart. The figurative admonition that man should leave things worldly and dwell in Christ is here taken literally, as Christ is contrasted with the world. His *skyn* is also opposed in its basic simplicity to the *gold* and *werdis wyn*, worldly joys or pleasures (1), which, ornate and expensive-seeming, are shown to be really deceptive. The image of the skin may also contain a reference to Christ as the lamb of God. To put on Christ's skin is to be lowly, meek, and away from *temporalia*.

The poem begins with a somewhat paradoxical statement—"Gold and al this werdis wyn / Is nouth but Cristis rode"—which acts as a premise for what follows. Here *rode* seems to mean "face or countenance" on the one hand and "cross" on the other, and *but* has the sense of "except" or "besides," with *nouth but* thereby meaning "only." The two lines would then support the following meanings: (1) that which is truly valuable (*gold*) and pleasurable (*wyn*) in this world is to be found only in Christ's countenance; (2) the world's gold and pleasures are nothing compared to what is contained in Christ; and (3) worldly wealth and joy must pale beside, and because of, the crucifixion. What all readings have in common is the idea that the desirable things of the world are necessarily replaced by Christ, and that, as St. Augustine phrased it, man should not value the creation at the expense of the Creator.

The apparent ambiguity continues in line 3, where *Cristis rode* is replaced by *Cristes skyn*, which acts to repeat the emphasis on Christ's person suggested by *rode* in its meaning of "face" and also to expand the crucifixion suggestion, inherent in *rode* and developed in line 4, "That ran so longe on blode." Lines 3–4 also present the opposite of lines 1–2, where the narrator was shown turning from this world. In lines 3–4, we see what he turns toward; and paradoxically

---

1. Brown, *Rel 14*, p. 276n.

this seems, at least on the surface, to be far less valuable than what he has given up. The attractive changes to the horrible, as *gold*—frequently referred to in the Middle Ages as "red gold"—becomes restated as *blode* (4), just as the *wyn* of the world changes to the *skyn* (3) of the world's victim and redeemer.

These lines also begin the statement of the narrator's action that, running through the next several lines, is the central and most developed sentence of the poem. Whereas the initial lines (1–2), along with the concluding lines (esp. 6, 8), are essentially statements of being, pivoting around the linking verb *is*, lines 3–5 contain the main verbs of action in the poem. These central lines show the narrator turning from his somewhat detached contrast of Christ and the world and affirming his commitment to Christ. Not only would he *ben clad in Cristes skyn*, that *ran* with blood—this being the most violent and dramatic action of the poem—he also would *gon* to Christ's heart and *taken* his dwelling there. This statement, while necessarily conditional, is not designed to weaken the verbs of action. It functions, in effect, as a statement of action, or, more accurately, as a statement of condition that may be translated into terms involving a shift from world to Christ. With the *then* clause of line 7, there is a suggestion of a fait accompli: even though the conditional tense remains, the mood seems to have become somewhat indicative, and the wished-for shift something of a fact.

A further paradoxical contrast appears in this section as Christ's body, especially his *skyn* and *herte*, is seen as a microcosm of the world, an analogy that had been implicit in the initial lines of the poem. The skin is something that can cover and shelter man, and the heart is large enough for man to make his dwelling there. As the narrator pauses to point out—wonderingly it would seem, though also delightedly—"Ther is a fulsum fode" (6), in Christ is abundant sustenance for all. In the single, simple, pathetic dying man of lines 3–4 is something nourishing and rewarding, apparently more so than all the gold and pleasures of the world. Paradoxically, what has seemed small is made large, and what has seemed large is rendered insignificant. Similarly, *blode* (4) and *fode* (6) act to suggest the blood and body of Christ, the Eucharist which is consumed by man in the Mass; and in this sense it may not be too farfetched to suggest that *wyn* (1) may also imply "wine" and lead to and contrast with Christ's blood.

The final lines (7–8) continue the large-small pattern, with their references to people who have no meaning because of the singular abundance of Christ who contains everything, even *kith or kyn*.

Similarly, the *fulsom*-ness of Christ makes things of this world seem *litel* to the narrator. His rejection of things and beings of this world is complete, and in the final lines he reaffirms his belief that in Christ, "ther is alle gode" (8). Because of the way the poem has developed, the last word *gode* would seem to include all beauty, wealth, shelter, food, family, and friends. It contains, as Christ does for the narrator, all the "goods" of the world and all that is really the Good. The poem is thus to be seen finally as a process of reevaluation, where the familiar and accepted are indirectly and metaphorically restated, so that the reader is left at the last line with a statement of what is real and worthwhile, a statement no longer paradoxical but clear.

Holding the poem together, as well as developing it, is a series of sound patterns that are as intricate as the patterns of stress and rhyme are simple. The alternating tetrameter and trimeter lines, essentially iambic with a running *ab* rhyme scheme, may suggest a popular origin for this lyric; but they reveal little about the complexity of the total work. The sound patterns tend to work along with the image patterns, reinforcing and linking key terms. The dominant sounds of the poem are /l/ and /d/, sometimes in combination, as in the initial word *gold*—which may be seen as reversed in *blode*, that which is here the opposite of gold. In like manner the initial *gold* and *al* are turned around, as it were, and restated at the end of the poem as *alle gode* (8), the sounds serving to unify the different morphemes, *gold-gode*. Most frequently, however, the /l/ and /d/ phonemes are separate, though at least one appears in each line. Whereas these sounds dominate the poem as a whole, they frequently produce only minor sound patterns: in line 1, for example, the /l/ appears in its dark or unreleased form; and, while a consonance is produced, it is necessarily minor, like the /d/ consonance in the same line. Dominant, on the other hand, is /w/, which appears in the alliterating *werdis wyn*. But except for *fulsom fode* (6) and *kith or kyn* (7) the lines in the poem show only imprecise alliteration—such as *clad in Cristes skyn* (3)—or none at all. The /o/ sounds, like /l/ and /d/, are present throughout the poem and create a pervasive, though not outstanding, pattern.

Interestingly, the only line without any noticeable assonance, consonance, or alliteration is the final line—"For ther is alle gode"—where the closest thing to a sound pattern is in the /ɔ-o/ of *for* and *gode*; but not only is this pattern imprecise, *for* is an unstressed syllable and clearly a minor word in the line. Perhaps the lack of sound pattern here is due to this line's functioning as the final explicit statement about Christ: it would thus seem proper for it to be without the connotative and poetic devices of the other lines. It is simple, denotative, and didactic, though, as has been seen, the final words *alle gode*, which are the substantive terms of the line, may refer back to and turn around the words *gold* and *al*, the initial substantives of the poem. In the last line, as in the first, the dominant phonemes are /o/ and /l/; and again the sounds link words which have stress and significance.

The eight lines of the lyric may well be without numerological significance, but at the same time, with eight being the main number of rebirth and rejuvenation,[2] a length of eight lines is appropriate for this poem, whose theme has to do with man's beginning the new life of Christ. The number of stresses per line, four alternating with three, may likewise function in terms of the numerical significance of world and spirit respectively. The four-stressed odd-numbered lines have to do with things of this world (1, 7) and with the wishes and actions of the narrator (3, 5), whereas the three-stressed even-numbered lines are all about Christ and his attributes. Sometimes the line about Christ is brought in to expand a thought, as in the dependent clause of line 4, although at other times it is intrusive or parenthetical, as in line 6. If such symbolism is present here, it is only one further example of the richness and complexity found in this lyric.

---

2. On eight, see, e.g., Augustine, *Epistolae*, LV.ix.17 (*PL* 33:212), and *De civitate Dei*, xv.20 (*PL* 41:463).

Adam lay ibowndyn, bowndyn in a bond,
Fowre thowsand wynter thowt he not to long;
And al was for an appil, an appil that he tok,
4   As clerkis fyndyn wretyn in here book.

Ne hadde the appil take ben, the appil taken ben,
Ne hadde neuer Our Lady a ben heuene qwen;
Blyssid be the tyme that appil take was,
8   Therfore we mown syngyn *Deo gracias!*

Sloane MS 2593, fol. 11.
Index, no. 117, p. 20; *Supplement*, p. 16.

Editions:
    Brown, *Rel 15*, no. 83, p. 120.
    Chambers and Sidgwick, no. 50, p. 102.
    Davies, no. 71, pp. 160–61.
    Stevick, *One*, no. 53, p. 98.

Criticism:
    Kane, p. 139.
    Speirs, pp. 65–66.
    Manning, *Wisdom*, pp. 6–7.
    Woolf, pp. 290–91.

ON THE SURFACE a naive, unsophisticated ballad-like piece, even revealing faulty meter—as in line 4—this lyric still has a compelling
quality that stems from its simple language and the combination of
its rhythms and sounds. It demonstrates how effectively religious
subject matter can be combined with popular verse techniques, producing an entity that retains characteristics of each without there
being any sort of wrenching or distortion. The theme of the *felix
culpa*, originally from the Easter liturgy, "O felix culpa, O necessari-
um peccatum ade," is itself a theological commonplace and a concept
frequently expressed in medieval writing. It does not, however, customarily appear in a setting like this, and it is rarely stated with such
poetic merit.

The poem, beginning with the fall of man, is concerned with the
result of this act and not with the act itself. Its first statement is of
Adam, held prisoner for at least four thousand years because of his
failure to obey God. This Adam acts as the representative of post-
lapsarian man, and his punishment is, in effect, that which is still
suffered by mankind. The verbs of all the independent clauses in the
first stanza, however, are in the past tense: the action is not of the
moment. Whereas we might expect the second stanza to use a present
tense that would contrast with the past state, the verbs actually
change from simple preterite to pluperfect tense. This shift gives an
unexpected reexamination of Adam's so-called crime. Because Adam
disobeyed God by taking an apple (apparently from Latin *malum*,
easily confused with *malus*, evil)—although the poem is without any
reference to his disobedience as such—he was punished. But had he
not taken the apple, things apparently would not have been better
for man.[1] What may justifiably be expected here is the traditional
contrast between Adam, the old man, and Christ, the new one. But
the contrast turns out to be between Adam and Mary, *Our Lady*
(11); and Christ is never even explicitly mentioned. The immediate
virtue of this unexpected relationship is that the poem is kept from
becoming a cliché: it is able to use a well-known subject but handle
it in a fresh way. Had the poem kept to the usual presentation of the
Adam-Christ contrast and developed this fully, it would only have
emphasized the obvious and the expected. As the poem exists, it
possesses the virtues of conciseness and understatement; and these

---

1. Woolf points out that the recurrence of this paradox may be explained
by its value "as a brief and neat denial of the controversial doctrine of Duns
Scotus that the Incarnation was predestined whether or not man fell" (pp. 290–
91).

serve to make it seem oversimplified, here a strength rather than a weakness.

The poem begins by directing our attention to Adam in his chains, a condition of bondage that acts as the focal point for what follows. And while we look, we may well feel a sense of both waste and frustration: it does not seem right that the taking of an apple should result in an imprisonment of four thousand years. Such a punishment seems unbelievable, though, says the poem, we have written authority for it—no less than what is *wretyn* in the *book* of the *clerkis* (4). We might suspect that in this ironic disbelief here is a hint of incredulity at the nature of divine justice, but such an impression fades with the examination in the second stanza of the real result and significance of the theft and of man's punishment for it. Had the apple not been taken, Mary would not have become queen of heaven (5-6). As Manning points out, the clerks' search for causes gives way to the poet's concern with effects.[2] And with Mary, it is suggested, comes Christ, redeemer of mankind in general and rescuer through his harrowing Hell, of Adam in particular. The poem is finally an affirmation of divine justice and order, the four thousand years traditionally being related to the four weeks of Advent before the birth of Christ. The lyric supports a belief that everything has turned out for the best, and the final *Deo gracias!* (8) removes all irony and doubt. The logic of the second stanza may be questionable, but we have finally no desire to question it. We are like children hearing a fairy tale that we fully accept. The piece creates and possesses its own logic and does not challenge us to answer its statements. Our response becomes a cheerful acceptance, as though we are glad to know that God is in his heaven and all is right with the world, with man, and with the past, present, and future of both.

As it is printed by most modern editors, the poem is in the form of sixteen short lines[3] instead of the eight longer ones given here and in Brown. When considered as a poem of sixteen lines, the piece seems less poetically adept: the odd-numbered lines then lack rhyme, the divisions of lines are occasionally artificial and awkward, and there is no real agreement about how to handle line 4—"As clerkis fyndyn wretyn in here book"—a line which seems to be metrically deficient.[4] In any case, the visual pattern of the poem, the way it appears to the reader's eye, is incidental to the construction. The

---

2. Manning, *Wisdom*, p. 7.

3. Chambers and Sidgwick, Davies, and Stevick.

4. Whereas Davies and Stevick both divide the line after *fynden*, Chambers and Sidgwick separate it after *wretyn*.

poem originated as a linguistic structure having audial not visual effect, and any visual presentation should be supported by audial evidence, a kind that seems to be lacking here.

The poem is comprised of several kernel sentences, generally in the form of short, one-line independent clauses, end-stopped and most often not connected by coordinating conjunctions. But each line is also linked in terms of rhymed couplets—though the rhyme of 1–2 is somewhat imprecise—with lines 1, 3, and 5 using the kind of phrasal repetition common in ballad literature. The result of such repetition is that each of these lines appears to make a double line, a tetrameter followed by a trimeter that echoes its content—again the rhythm associated with the ballad. These lines are also the most metrically pronounced, the most alliterative, and, at the same time, the fastest-moving in the poem, and tend to contrast with the more prosaic and metrically awkward lines, 2, 4, and 6, that follow and occur between them.[5] The phrasal repetition of these odd-numbered lines may not be precisely incremental, but it does serve to expand and develop the introductory thoughts found in them. While the second part of line 1 hardly gives new information to the first part—we already know that Adam was *ibowndyn*, and it is not much additional help to know that he was *bowndyn in a bond*—it still provides an emphasis on the punishment. Our attention is taken away from Adam and directed at what has happened to him. The second line then comments further on the duration of the duress, using Adam's view of his situation to create a somewhat ironic understatement: "Fowre thowsand wynter thowt he not to long."

The third line begins what, in terms of content, is actually the second part of the poem, proceeding from the taking of the apple, a fait accompli that is well recorded and known to all learned men. With the fifth line and the beginning of stanza 2, this thought is repeated as the examination of the action begins. But not only does this line refer to line 3, it also restates itself in the second or trimeter part of the line. The main difference between the first part, "Ne hadde the appil take ben," and the second, "the appil taken ben," is not in terms of expansion—there is no incremental repetition here at all—but of positive direction. That is, the act of taking is negated, as it were, in the first part of the line by the *ne hadde;* but the second part, lacking the term, may be seen as affirming that the apple has indeed been taken. Similarly, the *ne hadde,* at the beginning of the next line (6)

---

5. The concluding lines (7–8) are a different matter and will be discussed later.

not only echoes the earlier term but also introduces a phrase that contrasts with the previous line. The earlier statement (5) makes use of a subjunctive mood that may even suggest a negation of the taking, and, as we have understood the preceding stanza, we would be delighted if Adam had not taken the apple at all. Our impression is that the "then" clause which follows this "if" one will show us all the good things we would have had—freedom, for instance, the opposite of the state of bondage seen in the first stanza. But, surprisingly, the second *ne hadde* leads to another condition, one that we do not respond to with delight: "Ne hadde neuer Our Lady a ben heuene qwen." We would not want such a conditional statement as this to become an actual one. The slave Adam is contrasted with the queen Mary: as Adam created the cause for Christ to be born, so did Mary give birth to him. But at the same time, Adam may be viewed as leading to Mary.

Although such an interpretation may seem ambiguous, the problem lies mainly in attempting to state denotatively the connotative lines of the poem. The final couplet, however, removes the complexity and takes us from intellectual perplexity to faithful acceptance and praise of God and his will: "Blyssid be the tyme that appil take was, / Therfore we mown syngyn *Deo gracias!*" These lines also clearly shift the pronouns of the poem from the third person—the singular *he* representing Adam (2, 3) has led to the plural *here*, referring to the *clerkis* (4). But in the final line, with the shift to *we*—which may in a sense have been anticipated by *Our* in line 6—the audience is brought into the action of the lyric to participate in that which is happy and *blyssid*. Such participation is the opposite of what occurred in the first stanza of the poem where Adam stood alone. Even though mankind is necessarily linked to Adam and his fate, it is not an association we prize. But at the end of the poem we gladly join ourselves to Mary and through her to God. We are fortunate to have Mary to intercede for us, and, as we recognize our good luck, we can hardly do other than join the narrator in saying *Deo gracias!*

Sodenly afraide,
Half-waking, half-slepyng,
And gretly dismayde,
4   A wooman sate weepyng—

With fauoure in hir face ferr passyng my reason,
And of hire sore weepyng this was the enchesone:
Hir soon in hir lap lay, she seid, slayne by treason.
8 Yif wepyng myght ripe bee, it seemyd than in season.
        "Ihesu!" so she sobbid,
        So hir soone was bobbid,
        And of his lif robbid,
12   Saying thies wordis, as I say thee:
        "Who cannot wepe, come lerne at me."

I said I cowd not wepe, I was so harde-hartid.
Shee answerd me with wordys shortly that smarted:
16 "Lo, nature shall move thee, thou must be converted.
Thyne owne fadder this nyght is deed"—lo, thus she thwarted—
        "So my soon is bobbid,
        And of his lif robbid."
20   Forsooth than I sobbid,
        Veryfying the wordis she seid to me:
        "Who cannot wepe may lerne at thee."

"Now breke hert, I the pray! this cors lith so rulye,
24 So betyn, so wowndid, entreted so Iewlye;
What wight may me behold and wepe nat? Noon truly,
To see my deed dere soone lygh bleedyng, lo, this newlye."
        Ay stil she sobbid,
28   So hir soone was bobbed,
        And of his lif robbid,
        Newyng the wordis, as I say thee;
        "Who cannot wepe com lerne at me."

32 On me she caste hire ey, said, "See, mane, thy brothir!"
    She kissid hym and said, "Swete, am I not thy modir?"
    In sownyng she fill there, it wolde be non othir;
    I not which more deedly, the toone or the tothir.
36   Yit she revived and sobbid,
            So hire soon was bobbid
            And of his lif robbid.
40   "Who cannot wepe"—this was the laye;
    And with that word she vanysht away.

Rylands Lib., Manchester, MS 18932 (formerly Lat. MS 395), fols. 120–120v.
  Cf. Trinity Col. Camb. MS 1450, fol. 62v.

Index, no. 4189, p. 672; *Supplement*, p. 489.

Editions:
  Brown, *Rel 15*, no. 9, pp. 17–18.
  Greene, *EEC*, no. 161, p. 121.
  Stevick, *One*, no. 86, pp. 150–51.
    (Trin. Col. version) Furnivall, F., ed., *Hymns to the Virgin and Christ, EETS*
    OS 24 (London, 1887), pp. 126–27; Chambers and Sidgwick, no. 79,
    pp. 144–45.

EXISTING IN TWO MANUSCRIPT VERSIONS, this very interesting poem
presents a blend of alliterative and metrical techniques, dialogue and
narrative, and the dream and waking worlds. Indeed, through its initial four lines—which exist in one manuscript as two long lines—we
move into the poem *in medias res* and into the blends that comprise
it. These initial lines, separate from the four stanzas that follow, representing the actual body of the poem, act as a preface which runs on
into the first stanza. But at the same time, these lines are syntactically
awkward. The grammatical order would seem to indicate that the five
past and present participles occurring here function to modify *wooman* (4); she may well be described as *afraide* (1), as *half-waking,
half-slepyng* (2), as *gretly dismayde* (3); and she is clearly *weepyng*
(4). But several of these participles—especially those of lines 1–2—
also could refer properly to the narrator and, by implication, to the
audience of the poem that go with the narrator into a strange world
between consciousness and sleep. It is right for him and us to be *sodenly afraide*, for we do not know where we are or what is going to
happen in this twilight world. A tension thus exists at the beginning
that runs through the poem, reinforcing our realization that what we
are viewing is in no way a soothing courtly love vision.

In these first four lines we come upon a sight that acts as the focal
point for what follows, and as we respond to it we are caught up in its
action: it is not just a pageant or sign existing for our edification.
Consequently, in what follows, first in lines 5–6, we cannot help but be
struck by the sight of how beautiful the woman is and by the paradox
of how strange it is for her to be *sore weepyng* and still possess *fauoure in hir face*. Such a phenomenon is also beyond the narrator's
understanding—*ferr passyng my reason* (5)—but *reason* here is also
what is being gone beyond by the experience and the words of the
woman. Thus the scene is set for the study that follows: we see the
woman's sorrow and the reason for it, and feel the waste. Without
trying to stretch out or expand his allegorical picture, the poet would
appear to realize that we understand what the scene is about when
he states that the lady's dead son is *Ihesu* (9–10). But at the same
time, this name exists most immediately not in the context of her
naming her son or as an explanation of what is occurring. Rather, the
term functions as an exclamation, as though the lady in her sorrow is
calling on Jesus—who, ironically, is there dead in her arms. In the
Trinity College version the term is repeated at the beginning of line
18, again appearing to stand out as an expletive, but it is really unnecessary and makes the line metrically awkward.

When the short lines occur in stanza 1, we move from the narrative to a refrain that stresses the unfairness of Christ's death; then with the new longer lines, we are introduced to an additional theme that increases in importance as it is restated throughout the next stanzas: "Who cannot wepe, come lerne at me" (13). The main motif so far has been the lady's—that is, Mary's—weeping, and now weeping becomes a necessity for man. Not to weep is, as it were, to deny Christ and his death; the sacrifice would be negated if man remained *harde-hartid* (14). To weep is to have contrition, and contrition is the first step toward salvation. To weep is also to go beyond words, to let action be acknowledgment, and to go beyond *reason*.

With the second stanza, the narrator comes fully into the poem. He acts as representative of all who are *harde-hartid*, but the words of Mary smart him as he realizes that her dead son is his dead father: "Thyne owne fadder this nyght is deed" (17). As she says, "nature shall move thee, thou must be converted" (16). Not to be *converted* is to be *harde-hartid* and dry-eyed. If man is to be seen as a part of nature and not merely as a rent in her gown—as he was in Alan of Lille's well-known *Complaint of Nature*—he must acknowledge the bond that joins him to Jesus and recognize the blow to nature of Jesus' death and of man's hardheartedness. The last lines of the stanza bring the narrator even more into the poem as he becomes a surrogate for the weeping Mary, a witness to the power of both the weeping and Jesus' death. His act of sobbing (20) verifies, as it were, Mary's words. It functions to demonstrate, prove, and validate them. The Rylands Library reading—the given one—is far superior to the Trinity College version, which reads, "Verifying this wordis, seing to thee, / Who can not wepe com lerne at me." Although this pattern is the same as that in the previous stanza and in the succeeding one, the lines themselves are less dramatic and less meaningful than those in the Rylands version—"Veryfying the wordis she seid to me: / Who cannot wepe may lerne at thee" (21–22). Here the narrator enters the action in a new way, and becomes a Mary figure, acting not only as a proof of her words but also as an example to all of how they should respond to these words.

The opening lines of the next stanza could be a continuation of the narrator's response, although they turn out to be Mary's response. The method of the entire poem has involved an alternation of narrator and Mary, as in the four-line preface, where lines 1–2 were most relevant to the narrator and 3–4 most pertinent to Mary. The initial lines of both the first and second stanzas belong to the narrator. They show things from his point of view and concern his reaction to the vision. Then the focus shifts to Mary and to Jesus dead in her lap.

The short lines that follow in each stanza are concerned mainly with the death of Jesus, and the final longer lines act to bring everything together, as they contain references to both Mary and the narrator.

In stanza 3, however, the order tends to shift. This and the fourth stanzas begin with an action or statement by Mary that, though pertaining to and involving the narrator, really has no room for him. These stanzas are different from the first two where the narrator was brought, almost in spite of himself, into the action. The culmination of his place in the action of this poem comes at the end of stanza 2 when he weeps and becomes a model for others. What follows is mainly a development of Jesus' suffering. We know that Mary's son has been *slayne by treason* (7), but even with the restatement in the short lines of each stanza we do not discover the enormity of the crime until stanza 3. Although the narrator has wept, all of mankind must likewise weep; so now we see how the "corse lith so rulye, / So betyn, so wowndid, entreted so Iewlye" (23–24). The act is so cruel and unnatural that every *wight* or creature (25), that is, man along with all living things, can hardly help but respond with tears.

The culmination of the movement to making all realize the enormity of the crime comes in the final stanza when the narrator understands that the dead Jesus was also his *brothir* (32) and that Mary is therefore his own mother. Line 33 is somewhat ambiguous, for Mary's question, "Swete, am I not thy modir?" seems to be directed at both the dead man in her arms, whom she has just kissed, and the living man to whom she appears in this vision. The grief likewise inreases until Mary herself swoons (34) and then vanishes (40). The ending is not clear. The disappearance is neither because Mary has convinced mankind to weep nor because she has failed to do this. Rather, the action serves to give final recognition to the significance of this vision. If man will not weep after seeing such cruelty, so pathetic a death, and so fair a lady weeping for her dead son and finally fainting in her anguish, perhaps he will respond when he realizes the otherworldly nature of the speakers and that they exist only to show him the truth.

The direction taken by each stanza is revealed at the beginning of the penultimate line in each. The first stanza is an initial presentation, and there Mary is described as *saying thies wordis* (12); in stanza 2, the line is *verifying the wordis* (21), making clear what the narrator's tears have done; in stanza 3, it is *newyng the wordis* (30), narrowing the restatement and renewal contained in the stanza; and in stanza 4, the expression, *who cannot wepe* (39), with the implied continuation of the sentence, takes the place of the words and the statement about the words. The statement has come to stand for everything and needs no further describing or restating. But whereas Mary vanishes—"And with that word she vanysht away" (40)—so the word remains, as the poem demonstrates through its being; and as Christ is the word, so does he likewise remain. A rather complicated shifting of focus keeps the poem from fixing on any one thing or person, and the resultant shifting of attention makes the reader realize that many things are happening at once. The poem is about Mary's sorrow, which stems from Christ's death, and which leads to the narrator's sorrow. It relies heavily on tears and on an emotional reaction, but at the same time it uses this reaction to imply theological, ethical, and psychological questions, finally getting at the human understanding of and response to the Crucifixion, and the resultant contrition and recognition of the audience's own sins.

The rhythm of the poem is as complex as its stanzaic structure. The lines are by and large alliterative rather than metrical, even when there is no precise alliteration. The first four lines rhyme as a quatrain, *abab*, but they are two-stressed, with each line's having an indeterminate number of unstressed syllables and with there being no precise metrical patterning to the stresses. In these lines the prevalent sounds are the /s/ and /w/ consonants and the /ey/ vowel sounds. The long vocalic sound is especially drawn out, perhaps creating in conjunction with the consonants a feeling of grief and sorrow that is, as it were, built in. And these are also the main sounds of the four stanzas that follow. The first four long lines of each of the next stanzas are four-stressed, two stresses in each half line with a caesura in the middle, even though lines 17, 26, and 32 are slightly difficult to scan. The customary pattern in each half-line is an initial unstress followed by a stress, as though it were an iamb, with a reversed stress-unstress pattern at the end and with unstresses in between. The pattern is usually this—X/X|X/X||X/X|X/X—as though two amphibrachs were filling each half-line, although occasionally an extra unstress comes in. This pattern would seem to continue in the three short lines of each stanza, for even while occasionally appearing to be three-stressed, they seem finally to have the same kind of rhythm found in the four preceding long lines. But the pattern changes markedly in the final two lines of each stanza. In length different from all other lines, these also stand out by being much more regular in terms of conventional metrics. They are essentially iambic tetrameter—even though a couple begin with a trochee (12, 30), and even though the last line of the two is in each case more regular than the first.

The pattern seems to go from a rhythm full of unstresses—an active, rocking rhythm—to something calmer that slows down the stanzas at the end, giving at the same time a sense of pause or finality to each. This slowing down is aided by the masculine ending of the last two lines in the stanzas, as opposed to the feminine endings marking all the others. The rhyming sounds are here the drawn-out /ey/ sounds seen earlier within the initial quatrain, and as couplets they contrast with the four- and threefold repetition of sounds that precede them. The repetition of *sobbid, bobbid,* and *robbid*—in this order in three of the four stanzas—is certainly designed to emphasize the sorrow about Christ (*sobbid*), as well as his mistreatment (*bobbid*) and the waste brought about by his death (*robbid*). These words may also be viewed as onomatopoeic in that the stops /b/ and /d/ may seem to imitate or suggest the act of weeping.

The sense of frustration becomes most pronounced in the final line of the lyric. The vision has become so real to us—we have been so inundated with its sounds and sights—that the final line, "with that word she vanysht away," seems almost to describe something happening by magic. Nothing is left except the grief that man hopefully continues to feel. Such an ending emphasizes the supernatural significance of the scene and also keeps the poem from seeming overstated and too didactic, for with it we return to an awareness of the *sodenness;* and perhaps we too will be *afraide* because of what has occurred.

I wende to dede, knight stithe in stoure,
Thurghe fyght in felde i wane the flour;
Na fightis me taght the dede to quell—
4 I weend to dede, soth i yow tell.

I weende to dede, a kynge iwisse;
What helpis honor or werldis blysse?
Dede is to mane the kynde wai—
8 I wende to be clade in clay.

I wende to dede, clerk ful of skill,
That couth with worde men mare and dill.
Sone has me made the dede ane ende—
12 Beese ware with me! To dede i wende.

Brit. Mus. Cotton MS Faustina B. v.1, pt. 2, fol. ɪv.
Index, no. 1387, p. 219.

Editions:
   Brown, *Rel 15*, no. 158, pp. 248–49.
   Stevick, *One*, no. 87, p. 152.

Criticism:
   Oliver, pp. 107–08.

COMPELLING IN PART because the moment of the poem is the moment of death, these stanzas within the *contemptus mundi* tradition show how man's worldly activity has not prepared him for death. Even though he may prosper as warrior, monarch, or scholar, man is still helpless before death. Neither prowess, power, nor knowledge is sufficient to save him; and, willy-nilly, he will serve finally as an exemplum of the fate of mankind and as a warning to others that his end will be theirs. The initial phrase, "I wende to dede," which may be translated loosely as "I am on my way to death," acts to surprise us. With it we come upon the action not *in medias res* but *in terminis*, and we are likely to be taken aback by the immediacy of death. As the phrase is repeated throughout the poem, its implications grow and its effectiveness increases.

Ostensibly in the form of an apostrophe or a monologue addressed to knight, king, and clerk, the poem is also a record of the powers and limitations of the states represented metonymically by these figures (*denominatio*). The narrator appears as an authority on the various states referred to, and what follows the initial "I wende to dede" in each stanza may represent the person who is being addressed or may be in apposition to the *I* who is speaking. Both possibilities are likely and pertinent. The narrator is not only speaking to knight, king, and clerk; he has been all these things, and because he knows, he cannot be challenged as incompetent to speak. In the first stanza the narrator points out that being *stithe in stoure* (strong in battle, 1) does not enable one *the dede to quell* (3). The narrator also has *wane the flour* (2), and he knows that worldly combat is no preparation for killing death and that, so it would seem, mankind cannot defeat death. Similarly in stanza 2, in the role of king, he points out that whereas *honor* and *werldis blysse* (6) may seem to make man impervious to death, such is not the case at all: to be *clade in clay* (8) is man's fate. And finally in stanza 3, the *skill* (9) of the learned man is likewise shown to be inadequate and irrelevant when one is faced with the fact of death. Neither the logician, who through his words can deny the existence of death, nor the theologian, who asserts how death will die, can prevail.

In each of the three stanzas death is seen in a slightly different way. First, death is the all-powerful adversary of man, though, when called *the dede* (3), it may be more specifically identified as the Black Plague. Second, death is not a personification but a setting, as it were, the *kynde wai* (7), the path of all nature, including, to be sure, mankind. To be *clade in clay* (8) is more natural and, in a sense, more proper than to be dressed in expensive clothes, precious stones, or medals. And third, death appears as a state opposite to both life and man. It is a metamorphosis that everyone and everything undergoes, and in the change the living may be seen as becoming not only the dead but Death itself. Thus the narrator's words at the end of the poem, "Beese ware with me! To dede i wende" (12), may contain more than the restatement that he is dying and the charge that we should take note of his end. We have been made aware of man's fate throughout the three stanzas, but here may be the additional suggestion that we should "beware of" this man on his way to death. He stands out, different from the healthy and the thriving. His having been touched by death, makes him seem threatening to us, as though he were a surrogate for or microcosm of Death. If *wende* may also be viewed as meaning "change," this transformation would be all the more obvious; but in any case the suggestion is implicit.

This interpretation is reinforced by what follows the third stanza in another version of this poem, which may be termed *C* in contrast to the present version *A*. Eight additional lines serve to make clear the transformation of the narrator and his implicit identification with Death:

> Be ye wele now warre with me!
> My name then is ded;
> May ther none fro me fle,
> That any lyfe gun led—
> Kynge, kasere, theyn, no knyght,
> Ne clerke that cane on boke rede,
> Beest, ne foghel, ne other wyght—
> Bot i sal make tham dedde.[1]

What in *A* is implicit and ambiguous becomes explicit here. A Dr. Jekyll–Mr. Hyde kind of transformation appears to have taken place, and now, not only is the narrator's name *ded*, he acts also to kill all who live. At the same time, this expansion is irrelevant: while clarifying, it also makes what was tantalizing in *A* appear overstated and tedious, especially in its unnecessary repetition and catalogue of how no one can escape death.

Such a poem as this has an effectiveness that is built in, as it were, and that is difficult to remove. But *C* lacks the understatement of *A* that keeps the given open-ended, constantly present, and at the same time constantly strange. An implicit drama develops throughout *A*, and without overt didacticism the monologue reveals a personal tone

---

1. Normalized from Stowe MS 39, fol. 32; printed in Brown, *Rel 15*, p. 250.

that makes its commonplace subject fresh and intriguing. The constant stanzaic structure of mainly end-stopped couplets in iambic tetrameter functions to give an epigrammatic or apothegmatic quality to the lines and to keep them somewhat formal, at least more so than would have been the case if the structure had been in terms of, say, alternating four-stressed and three-stressed lines employing a ballad rhyme scheme. Such a popular form would make unconvincing and even ridiculous the references to the noble and learned occupations. The treatment given here is, however, very appropriate to the subject and works well with the other verse techniques of the poem. Repetition found in phrases, words, rhymes, and stress patterns is the norm here; and the movement to death is emphasized and made to seem inexorable—at least if man keeps to the life that is subject to death.

Some of the patterns of repetition are formal variations of *repetitio* and deserve comment. The phrase "I wende to dede," appearing with variations at the beginning and end of each stanza, is, insofar as it approaches being a refrain, similar to the rhetorical device of epimone, or even, as an echoic device, epanalepsis; and the inversion of the phrase in the last line of the poem may be seen as an instance of chiasmus (*commutatio*). The sense of repetition is supported by the word *dede* which appears in three of the four lines of each stanza, except for the second, where death is euphemistically referred to as being *clade in clay* (8). But even while the poem emphasizes death, it is far from being a deliberation on the subject. In fact, just the opposite would seem to be true. Man is asked to take more notice of death than he ever has and, realizing that this will be his end, to prepare accordingly so as to defeat it. The stressed sounds /w/ and /d/ of the phrase "I wende to dede," along with /k/ and, in the first stanza, /f/, are the dominant sounds of the poem. While these phonemes do not seem to have any special significance in themselves or create any particular effect, they help to unify the poem and hold it together.

The poem seems to have been popular, existing, according to Brown, in three versions, the other two—B^2 and C—differing from A mainly in reversing the order of stanzas, although, as has been seen, C also adds some lines at the end. In B the references are to king, clerk, and knight in that order; and in C to clerk, king, and knight, respectively. The order in A seems preferable, with its movement from the highest things of this active life to the contemplative life; or, to approach it in another way, the movement is from fighting in the world, and glorying in it, to musing about it, resulting finally in something of

---

2. Brit. Mus. Addit. MS 37,049, fol. 36; printed in Brown, *Rel 15*, p. 249.

a detachment but not one that can save man. The *clerk ful of skill* is here no ideal, for with his words he can only *mare and dill* (10), an ambiguous phrase probably meaning something like "mar and make dull." That is, *skill* becomes a pejorative, and the words of the man who is *ful of skill*, perhaps instead of God and holiness, can only lead other men astray. In B *mare and dill* appears as *mete and stylle*, in other words "checkmate and subdue"; and in C the reading is *mate men at will*. Although these two readings may be clearer than that in A, they are less applicable; for the words seem out of place in the clerk's mouth and more properly refer to death, traditionally said to "checkmate and still" man. Opposed to false acting and false speaking are the words of the narrator, who presumably can be believed since he is on his way to death.

But the narrator's explicit message is that man cannot hope to prevail over death, at least not in his roles of knight, king, and clerk. There would seem to be some other way, although the poem chooses not to go into this matter. To be viewed properly, the lyric must be seen as presenting something quite different from an *Ubi sunt?* or *Ubi erunt?* theme—there is no dwelling here on the snows of yesteryear—and something more than thoughts on a *momento mori*. It may be viewed as a *danse macabre* of sorts, a motif very popular in the late Middle Ages, and one customarily using such figures as knight, king, and learned man to show the fall of the mighty, the *casibus virorum illustrium*.[3] Another refrain common in fifteenth-century English verse is *Timor mortis conturbat me*, where the fear of death is seen gnawing at the speaker; and this seems to provide a fair statement of the theme of this lyric. If man fears death sufficiently, he will do something about it, something having nothing to do with the power, glory, and knowledge of the world.

---

3. See, e.g., the woodcuts by Hans Holbein (*Holbein's Dance of Death and Other Woodcuts,* New York, 1947, passim).

I syng of a myden
That is makeles;
Kyng of alle kynges
4   To here sone che ches.

He came also stylle
Ther his moder was,
As dew in Aprylle
5   That fallyt on the gras.

He cam also stylle
To his moderes bowr,
As dew in Aprille
12   That fallyt on the flour.

He cam also stylle
Ther his moder lay,
As dew in Aprille
16   That fallyt on the spray.

Moder and mayden
Was neuer non but che—
Wel may swych a lady
20   Godes moder be.

Bodl. Sloane MS 2593, fol. 10v.
Index, no. 1367, p. 216; *Supplement*, p. 164.

Editions:
> Brown, *Rel 15*, no. 81, p. 119.
> Chambers and Sidgwick, no. 54, p. 107.
> Davies, no. 66, p. 155.
> Stevick, *One*, no. 54, p. 99.

Criticism:
> Kane, pp. 161–65.
> Spitzer, *ArL*, pp. 152–63.
> Speirs, pp. 67–69.
> Manning, Stephen, "I syng of a myden," *PMLA*, 75 (1960), 8–12; repr. in *Wisdom*, pp. 158–67.
> Raw, Barbara C., "'As Dew in Aprille,'" *MLR*, 55 (1960), 411–14.
> Copley, J., "'I Syng of a Myden,'" *N&Q*, 207 (1962), 134–37.
> Stevick, *MP*, p. 116.
> Woolf, p. 287.

PROBABLY THE MOST DISCUSSED AND ADMIRED of the Middle English lyrics, this piece has also been termed "the finest example of the poetry of wit in the Middle English period.[1] In some ways, however, such praise and concern seem extreme, not because the poem is unworthy, but because there exist so many other works at least as good. "I syng of a myden" is metrically simple, its structure is uncomplicated, and its imagery, which has received most of the attention, is almost overtly allegorical. That is, the poem exists as a kind of simple riddle in the form of an oblique statement: from its opening line, it asks its audience to consider the paradox of the virgin birth; and while it never actually states that it is about Mary or Christ, its middle three stanzas act as hints of its real subject. But at the same time as we may qualify our praise of this poem, there is no denying its real merit. The problem is that through existing as a *pièce célèbre* it has gone beyond being a touchstone for demonstrating the quality of Middle English lyrical poetry and become the representative, as it were, of this poetry.

Existing superficially as a courtly love lyric about a *kyng* (3) and a *lady* (19), the poem also appears, initially at least, to be a song. In the first line the narrator announces that he will *syng* of something profound—"a myden / That is makeles" (2–3), but the simplicity of what follows seems to belie the complexity of the subject. The succeeding lines should doubtless be understood as being in the narrator's voice and as having a personal significance to him, although the narrator is here a spokesman for mankind, and what he sings is of universal interest and relevance. To sing of something is to celebrate that thing and to indicate that it is significant and worthy of being voiced and heard. But ironically the *I syng* is followed by an emphasis on silence. The singing is the only action of the poem that has any sound to it and contrasts most noticeably with the *stylle* of stanzas 2–4, indicating the way Christ came to Mary, and also with the silent falling of the dew in these same stanzas. From this almost epic-like beginning the poem becomes a whisper of sorts, and the heroic deeds we might expect to be its content are replaced by the sound of silence, peace, and fulfillment. The *kyng of alle kynges* (3) is surprisingly gentle and non-threatening in his actions.

The most significant word in the first stanza is *makeles* (2). The *myden*, with which this word alliterates, is properly *makeles* in the sense of being without a mate. But although this connection seems both likely and proper, the resulting emphasis on virginity only heightens the paradox created by the next two lines, where, unexpec-

---

1. Manning, *Wisdom*, p. 158.

tedly, we find that she has a son. A second relevant meaning of *make-les* is "matchless": the *myden* is special and worthy of being singled out as subject of the song. In this sense, the word leads to, instead of contrasting with, what appears in the next line: it is appropriate for her to be presented in connection with the *kyng of alle kynges*. Also the phrase refers obliquely to the maiden herself, by suggesting that she is to be viewed as queen of all queens, and serves to heighten her own nobility by further stressing her uniqueness, something brought out explicitly in the last stanza: "Moder and mayden / Was neuer non but che" (17–18). A third possible significance for *makeles* may stem from Latin *macula*, in the sense that to be *makeles* is to be *sine macula* or without stain. According to the Immaculate Conception, Mary, unlike other mortals, was viewed as born without the stain of original sin. In terms of this suggestion, *makeles* again refers back to *myden*, reinforcing and emphasizing it, and developing the meaning of Mary's purity.[2]

The fourth line—"To here sone che ches"—culminates the developing paradox of this stanza. We find not only that the maiden has a son who is, wondrously, the king of all kings, but also that she chose this king to be her son. Two points are involved here. First, there is a reversal of powers, in that the king seems to be guarded by her; second, we see her making the necessary choice that results in the king's being her son. Even though she is a maiden, with all the concomitant associations of meekness, humility, and passivity, she is presented as the active force of the poem. Spitzer cites a thirteenth-century poem, "Nu this fules singet hand maket hure blisse," that contains two lines quite similar to the first stanza of this poem: "Of on ic wille singen that is makeles, / The king of halle kinges to moder he hire ches."[3] While this is much more prosaic than "I syng of a myden," the main difference between the two passages is that the earlier one presents Mary as passive, as having been chosen by the king.

A further ambiguity may lie in the phrase *to here sone* (4). As we have been viewing it so far, it means "as her son"; and such would seem to be its intended meaning. But *here* may function as a pronoun as well as a possessive adjective, and, notwithstanding the slightly different phonological value of /o/, *sone* may be not "son" (OE *sunu*) but the adverb "soon" (OE *sóna*), meaning in Middle English "immediately" or "right away." If this were the reading, the following verb *ches* would be even stronger, perhaps containing the suggestion

---

2. Cf. the Middle English *Pearl*, l. 780; and Speirs, p. 69.

3. Spitzer, *ArL*, p. 159. The poem is printed in Brown, *13*, no. 31, p. 55, ll. 3–4. Lines 19–20 also resemble the last stanza. See also Davies, pp. 14–15.

of "took," the working out, as it were, of the choosing. Lines 3 and 4 would then mean something like "She quickly took the king of all kings to her," adding further to the paradox but leading directly to what is contained in the next three stanzas, where it is stated that the *He*, the king of all kings, comes to his mother. After all, the king is both creator and created, he who implanted the seed in Mary and he who was born of her. This paradox would then act as the male equivalent to the one stated in the last stanza, where the subject of the poem is described as both *moder and mayden* (17).

The first and last stanzas together act as a frame for the immediate dramatic action of the poem, which takes place in the three middle stanzas. But this action is also incongruously the opposite of action. The coming of the king to his mother is like no customary royal progress or entry. It is like something one does not know until it is there —like the dew that falls on the ground. And as has been seen the key word describing the way the king *cam* is the adverb *stylle*. To come *stylle* is first to negate somewhat the action of coming. *He cam* follows immediately the action of Mary, *che ches* (4); but with *stylle* added, it seems subordinated to and even weaker than her action. There is none of the fanfare associated with the king and none of the dominance associated with the male. This is Mary's poem, and throughout it she is in control.[4]

The term *stylle* is appropriate to the night in which Christ was conceived, just as it is to the time of his birth: the silent night of Christmas eve is found in several medieval sources.[5] Moreover, the word of God was seen as coming to the earth in a similar way, as in the apocryphal Wisdom of Solomon (18:14–15), which describes how the almighty word leaped down from heaven "while all things were in silence, and the night was in the midst of her course."[6] A time of stillness was apparently appropriate for such an action, for stillness was also seen as denoting freedom from concupiscence.[7] It would seem that by coming *stylle*, the king would not stain Mary or make her in any way less than *makeles*. Also, as Manning points out, "the silence is reverent—both fearing and ineffable. Perhaps, too, there is a suggestion of the dual nature of God according to some commentators, a

---

4. Spitzer refers to the "inherent solemnity" of the three central stanzas, to "a *rallentando* quality which forces us to linger on their content: on the poet's simple assertion that Christ came to earth as a *natural* phenomenon comparable to the dew in April" (p. 153).

5. Davies, pp. 334–35, cites, e.g., the *Sarum Missal.*

6. See also Davies, p. 335, and Manning, *Wisdom*, p. 163.

7. See, e.g., Amadeus of Lausanne, *De Maria Virginea Matre*, III (PL 188:1316–17), and Davies, p. 335.

paradox of tranquility and activity—'perfect stillness, perfect fecundity,' according to John Ruysbroeck."[8]

With the father-son king's coming three times to Mary, there is a primary emphasis on the process, the creative act itself, not on the product of the act. We see Mary becoming, as it were, the *moder* she is thrice said to be. As the passage describing the action repeats itself —the threefold reiteration suggesting an incantation—there is an increasing sense of stillness and awe. The stress on the number three is itself functional, for in terms of medieval numerology it suggests the presence of the Trinity—as though it were the Trinity that comes to Mary—and, moreover, symbolizes things spiritual as opposed to things physical or earthly. The hint of earthiness in these central stanzas is in some ways negated by the insistence on this number. Still, one cannot deny that a sensuousness develops through the three stanzas. In stanza 2 the king comes to where his mother was, an innocent enough statement; in stanza 3 he comes to his mother's *bowr* (bedroom, 10); and in the fourth stanza the suggestiveness increases as he comes to where she *lay* (14). The point of the coming is made clear as we become increasingly aware that the stanzas are describing a typical meeting between lovers; but we know that this meeting is special. The movement is from the traditional garden (of love) to the bower (of bliss) to the spray—that which is the first fruit of love and the creative act.

The simile dominating these central stanzas "As dew in Aprille, / That fallyt on the . . . " continues the understatement and the sense of humility found in the first stanza. The image also relates the *myden* to nature and natural processes of life and rejuvenation, and serves to explain in passing how Mary can be both *moder and mayden*. Dew is a traditional symbol of the Holy Spirit and of divine grace, this identification being based on such biblical passages as Judges 1:37–40, about Gideon's fleece. The twelfth-century preacher, Peter Celensis, writes, as Manning has pointed out and translated, "Dew cools, makes fecund, moistens, penetrates, cleanses, enters silently, pre-announces the heat and serenity of the day."[9] The dew is literally that which nightly freshens the world and gives it continuing life. The impregnation of Mary resembles this, and so does the coming of Christ, who will act to purify man and the world. The dew, moreover, is described as falling—a word lacking any force or determination, and be-

---

8. Manning, *Wisdom*, p. 163; the reference to Ruysbroeck is to *De vera contemplatione*, XII.

9. Peter Celensis, "In Annuntiatione Domina," VI (*PL* 202:721); Manning, *Wisdom*, p. 162.

ing quite different from the action of Mary when she *ches* (4). The dew is almost helpless, but in its falling it causes nature to thrive and grow.

The April setting of this action is significant in a similar way. Just as the dew rejuvenates the earth for the coming day, so is April to be identified with the morning of life. In the medieval world view the earth was thought to have been created in mid-March, and Spring was seen as representing the first months of the year. April is also the traditional month of showers, and as is well known from the beginning of Chaucer's *Canterbury Tales*, "Aprill with hire shoures soote" pierces the parched land and creates life. It is the time of love and procreation, when all of nature participates in creation. The king who is coming is in one sense this kind of life force. April, the dawn of life, is also the first month of Mary's pregnancy, suggesting the new life to come with Christ. Mary is like the earth that receives the dew, and she is properly described in terms of *gras* (8), *flour* (12), and *spray* (sprig, 16).

These words are the most significant variations in the incremental repetition of the central three stanzas. Manning sees the grass as representing humility, the flower as chastity, and the sprig as fecundity.[10] Whether or not we agree with this particular signification, we can hardly doubt that there is a progression in the images, perhaps from the commonplace and general, the grass, to the beautiful and special, the fruit of the blossom or sprig. While all three terms are applicable to Mary, the one most frequently used in reference to her is *flour*. She is traditionally described as "flower of chastity" (*flos castitatis*) and "flower of virginity" (*flos virginitatis*), though *spray* may also function as an English translation of Latin *virga*, which could have been confused with or suggestive of *virgo*, virgin. Most likely, however, the *gras*, *flour*, and *spray* have different reference points. That is, *gras* may be used mainly to express the simile and mean literally earth or figuratively the world that will be cleansed and made healthy through the coming of Christ; *flour* may be the particular reference to Mary and to her role in this creative, fructifying act; and *spray* may refer most to Christ, the growth that is the result of the act.

The final stanza of the poem is most like the first one and functions as a reiteration of the paradox and as a relatively explicit statement of the real subject of the poem. Here Mary is identified as *Godes moder*, and this is the answer to the riddle that has been sung. She is *moder*

---

10. Manning, *Wisdom*, p. 165.

and mayden, and only *swych a lady* as she can be both. The term
lady emphasizes her nobility, and is also appropriate since Mary is
customarily referred to as "Our Lady," and since the etymon of the
name "Mary" was believed to have been the Aramaic word for
"lady".[11] By the final line there should be no doubt that this is clearly
Mary's poem. Her attributes and name mark the poem; the dominant
alliterative sound is /m/, seen mainly in such words referring to Mary
as *myden, moder* (and their repetitions), as well as in *makeles.* And
Manning is surely right in pointing out that the five stanzas of the
poem refer to the symbolic number most associated with Mary. It is
the number of her joys and was seen as a number found everywhere
in Christian doctrine. It is, as Irenaeus, for instance, makes clear, the
number of letters in Latin *Soter* (savior), *Pater* (father), and *Agape*
(grace); and, having long been a holy number in Eastern Christianity, it came into the West signifying something circular, spherical,
and without end, like the pentangle or five-pointed star.[12]

Similarly, although the line division of the poem is moot, each
two-line unit is composed of five stresses, two alternating with three,
though in Brown's edition, where the poem is presented in ten long
lines, each line utilizes five stresses. In any case, as the rhyme shows,
there are two basic syntactic units per stanza, and each contains
five stresses. In like manner the total number of lines may be functional. Ten, Brown's number, is a traditional number signifying perfection, but twenty, the number of lines found in the Sloane MS and
in most modern editions, seems even more pertinent. Twice ten, it
also signifies perfection, but one that takes longer to come about. And
according to some commentators such as St. Augustine and Cassi-
odorus, twenty suggests the time of service, the time that comes between the promise, as it were, and the fulfillment.[13] This number
symbolism demonstrates further that everything in the poem seems
designed to create a certain view of Mary: she is its subject, and she
provides the basic materials for the complex artistic statement. But
everything is also kept simple on the surface—simple, uncluttered,
and, at the same time, universally suggestive.

---

11. Jerome, *De nominibus Hebraicis* (*PL* 23:886).

12. Irenaeus, *Contra Haereses,* II.24.4 (*PG* 7:794); Manning, *Wisdom,* p.
167.

13. Augustine, *Quaestionum in Heptateuchum,* IV.ii (*PL* 34:718); Cas-
siodorus, *Expositio in Psalterium,* XX (*PL* 70:152). Stevick also points out that
the structuring of the poem is clearer if it is read as being in couplets (*MP,*
p. 115).

Swarte-smekyd smethes, smateryd wyth smoke,
Dryue me to deth wyth den of here dyntes!
Swech noys on nyghtes ne herd men neuer:
4 What knauene cry and clateryng of knockes!
The cammede kongons cryen after "Col! col!"
And blowen here bellewys that al here brayn brestes:
"Huf, puf!" seyth that on, "Haf, paf!" that other.
8 Thei spyttyn and spraulyn and spellyn many spelles,
Thei gnauen and gnacchen, thei gronys togydere,
And holdyn hem hote wyth here hard hamers.
Of a bole hyde ben here barm-fellys;
12 Here schankes ben schakeled for the fere-flunderys.
Heuy hamerys thei han that hard ben handled,
Stark strokes thei stryken on a stelyd stokke:
"Lus, bus! Las, das!" rowtyn be rowe.
16 Sweche dolful a dreme the deuyl it todryue!
The mayster longith a lityl and lascheth a lesse,
Twyneth hem tweyn, and towchith a treble.
"Tik, tak! Hic, hac! Tiket, taket! Tyk, tak!
20 Lus, bus! Lus, das!"—Swych lyf thei ledyn!
Alle clothemerys, Cryst hem gyue sorwe!
May no man for brenwaterys on nyght han hys rest!

Brit. Mus. Arundel MS 292, fol. 71v.
Index, no. 3227, p. 513; *Supplement*, p. 358.

Editions:
    Robbins, *Sec*, no. 118, pp. 106–07.
    Sisam, pp. 169–70.
    Davies, no. 115, p. 213.

Criticism:
    Speirs, pp. 94–95.

As THE EARLIEST sustained onomatopoeic effort extant in English, this poem has frequently been singled out for praise. And even though its style has been called "generally unsuitable for lyric poetry,"[1] the poem has also been termed "a magnificent example of realism in verse."[2] While it may give the impression of being a fascinating oddity, it is also a well-formed and effective poem.

In the presence of such pronounced alliteration, it would be gratuitous to examine the sound patterns, though it may be pointed out that the alliterative four-stressed lines make no sustained or consistent use of a caesura. While some lines exhibit a natural and pronounced pause ("Thei gnauen and gnacchen, thei gronys togydere," 9), others seem to force a caesura ("And holdyn hem hote wyth here hard hamers," 10). Furthermore, the alliteration may be described as being of three types: first, that in which all four stressed syllables alliterate ("Swarte-smekyd smethes, smateryd wyth smoke, / Dryue me to deth wyth den of here dyntes," 1–2); second, that where, even though one stress may not alliterate, there exists a sufficient number of unstressed syllables containing the alliterating sound to make it appear as though it were permeating the line ("Of a bole hyde ben here barm-fellys," 11); and third, that where two sounds alliterate, sometimes by twos ("Here schankes ben schakeled for the fereflunderys," 12, with the /š/ being followed by /f/) and other times alternately ("'Huf, puf!' seyth that on, 'Haf, paf!' that other," 7, where /h/ or /p/ alternates with /o/). In such lines as this last one, that use reduplicated sounds, the stress seems to be mainly on the first element, here on *huf* and *haf* rather than on *puf* and *paf*. Such is clearly the case in "'Lus, bus! Las, das!' rowtyn be rowe" (15), a line also alliterating in pairs. If the stresses in the first half-line were on *bus-das* instead of *lus-las*, there would be no alliteration. A similar line is 20, where the identical sounds appear again ("Lus, bus! Lus, das!'–Swych lyf thei ledyn!"), although here the /l/ is dominant in all four stresses. By implication, it would seem that when the initial syllable of a line alliterates, that syllable is to be stressed. Thus, the completely echoic line 19 would probably be stressed as follows: "Tík, tak! Híc, hac! Tíket, taket! Týk, tak!"

It is curious that alliteration dominates all the lines until the last two, which would seem to be stressed as follows: "Álle clóthemerys, Crýst hem gyue sórwe! / May nó man for brénwaterys on nýght han hys rést" (21–22). Whereas assonance and consonance are clearly

---

1. Davies, p. 34.
2. Robbins, *Sec*, p. 265n.

present in these lines, alliteration is not at all so pronounced as in earlier lines. Such a change is likely purposeful and may be designed to allow the verse to trail off or to produce a curse that can stand out by its use of language which is relatively ordinary and stress which is relatively unemphasized in a context revealing elaborate sounds and driving stresses.

The smiths here described are hardly in the image of Tubalcain, the biblical smith frequently regarded as the inventor of music; for their cries and noises are cacophonous rather than harmonious. Especially functional in creating discord are the sibilants combined with other consonants such as /sm/ (1), /sp/ (8), /š/ (12), and /st/ (14), which may be seen as giving a sense of hissing and as working with the dentals /d/ (2, 16) and /t/ (18, 19) to suggest spitting. A harsher gutteral sound is produced by the voiceless palatal /k/ (4, 5, 21) and by the voiced palatal /g/ (9), both of which may be close to glottal sounds. These dental and palatal phonemes are all stops, suggesting a lack of smoothness; they are supported by the bilabial stop /b/ (6, 11) and by the nasals that permeate the poem but that are dominant in line 3. The resultant audial pattern is disruptive and noxious, and works hand in hand with the frightening visual scene to produce an effect that is skillful and without overstatement.

Such sounds, moreover, as *huf, puf* and *haf, paf* (7), *lus, bus! las, das* (15), or *lus, das* (20)—though the *u* may be an error—as well as the other echoic sounds, function not only to show the sounds of the bellows and of the hammer on the anvil but also to suggest the bestiality of the blacksmiths who, as they appear in this portrait, are noticeably dehumanized. From the beginning the smiths are seen as demonic creatures, as black men figuratively associated with death: "Swarte-smekyd smethes, smateryd wyth smoke, / Dryue me to deth" (1–2). They then appear to be subhuman: along with the huffing and puffing, "Thei spyttn and spraulyn and spellyn many spelles, / Thei gnauen and gnacchen, thei gronys togydere" (8–9). Dressed in their aprons of *bole hyde* (11), they work at night in a setting of fire and sparks (*fere-flunderys*, 12), creating discord. Noise, confusion, and even chaos are dominant and make us able to appreciate the narrator's attitude toward his subject: "Sweche dolful a dreme the deuyl it todryue!" (16). There is no wonder that he concludes with the curse, "Alle clothemerys, Cryst hem gyue sorwe!" (21). These unnatural-seeming, fearful-looking black men, working at night in their fiery forge, seem like representatives or manifestations of the devil; and the setting itself appears as a kind of hell.

The unnaturalness associated with the blacksmiths reaches a cli-

max of sorts in the last two lines, where they are termed *clothemerys*
(horse clothers, 21) and *brenwaterys* (water burners, 22). These
words, found nowhere else in the English language, suggest the blacksmiths' unnatural activities. The term *brenwaterys* in particular suggests that they are doing something both miraculous and destructive.
The phenomenon of burning the water by thrusting white hot iron into
it is seen as destructive, and the impression is that the blacksmiths,
through such unnatural practices, are reversing the processes of nature. In the Middle Ages blacksmiths were frequently seen in terms
of sin and deviltry and were even explicitly identified with the devil.
In a revelant analogy in the *Fasciculus morum* (fourteenth century)
the devil is said to entice men to the sin of lechery "in the manner of
a blacksmith who, when he is unable to manage the iron as he would
like, puts it on the fire and blows on it. So the devil, when he is unable
to control man as he would like, first inflames him with the fire of
sensuality." The various ways the devil manipulates man are then
listed and in each case related to the work of a smith. In conclusion,
the text explains how, through such manipulating, the devil bends
man to his will, "and with his hammers of various suggestions he
works the hard and obstinate heart on his forge, making of it what he
pleases."[3]

The important thing in understanding this poem is not that the
details, "drawn from eye and ear . . . must be direct from experience,"[4]
but rather than the picture given in this ostensibly secular poem is
more than accidentally suggestive of devils and hell. When we read
it, it is as though we have entered *in medias res* a typical medieval
vision like the *Vision of Tundale* or *St. Patrick's Purgatory*, and are
both witnessing and in part suffering some of the punishments of the
damned. But the nightmare quality is relieved by, or at least juxta-
posed against, the exaggeration that results from various sound patterns and the profuse echoic language. It is not that the blacksmiths
are being humorously berated and castigated here—as they frequently
were in the Middle Ages[5]—or at least such criticism is not a dominant
issue in this poem. Rather, we see hell being created in human terms,

---

3. *Fasciculus morum*, VII.5 (Rawlinson MS C. 670, fol. 144). Such an identification is reinforced by the scene found in many medieval visions of hell of the
valle fabrorum, the pit of smiths, where the devils are presented as blacksmiths
who torment the souls of sinners with their instruments. See, e.g., the *Vision of
Tundale* and the references given in Edmund Reiss, "Daun Gerveys in the
Miller's Tale," *PLL*, 6 (1970), 119–20.

4. Davies, p. 350.

5. See, e.g., the complaints about the nightly din of blacksmiths in the
fourteenth century, noted in E. P. Kuhl, "Daun Gerveys," *MLN*, 29 (1914), 156.

and human activities being defined symbolically in terms of the demonic. At the same time, the implied solution suggests the opposite of these blacksmiths and their noise. The peace, tranquility, and harmony traditionally associated with paradise, as well as the life of light, are implicit in this sense. The good man may hope for an eternity of the opposite of what is seen and heard here, but the sinner will know forever only such chaos and cacophony.

General Index

Index of First Lines